THE WHITE HOUSE: CELEBRATING TWO HUNDRED YEARS 1800–2000

WHITE HOUSE HISTORICAL ASSOCIATION   WASHINGTON, D.C.

WHITE HOUSE HISTORICAL ASSOCIATION STAFF

CONTENTS

4

Foreword

Several days after a presidential election, fiercely disputed and ultimately not settled for 35 days, President and Mrs. William J. Clinton hosted a historic dinner at the White House. Held on November 9, 2000, in cooperation with the White House Historical Association, the formal event celebrated the 200th anniversary of the home and office of the president of the United States. It was a remarkable and memorable evening that witnessed how the White House proved again to be a symbol of unity. While the nation struggled with the uncertain outcome of the election, President and Mrs. Clinton and their special guests— Lady Bird Johnson, President and Mrs. Gerald R. Ford, President and Mrs. Jimmy Carter, and President and Mrs. George Bush—gathered to honor the house and to reflect on the common ground of their contributions to its history. Unfortunately, President and Mrs. Ronald Reagan were unable to attend because of his illness. The speeches given that evening had a special resonance and importance, as the presidential election was of great concern to the nation. This anniversary publication documents the historic remarks made that evening and records the activities that surrounded the commemoration of the 200th anniversary of John and Abigail Adams's moving into the White House.

This book also represents a coming of age for the White House Historical Association, which was founded in 1961. I began my work with the association 40 years ago when Dr. Melville B. Grovesnor, then president and editor of the National Geographic Society, called a meeting to organize a White House guidebook project. Only a few days earlier, Dr. Grosvenor had enthusiastically accepted a request of the newly formed association for the National Geographic Society to produce the guidebook; it was to be done as a public service. At the time I was an illustrations editor for *National Geographic*. Our project team was given just three weeks to design the book and to present a layout to Mrs. John F. Kennedy for her review and approval. Just six months later, on July 4, 1962, the book went on sale at the White House. It was wildly popular, selling out the first edition within 90 days.

In 2001, the 21st edition of the guidebook was published. Since 1962 the association's publication program has grown to include *The Presidents of the United States, The First Ladies, The Living White House,* and *The White House Garden* and to sponsor major scholarly works, *The President's House, Art in the White House: A Nation's Pride, White House History,* and *The White House: Its Historic Furnishings and First Families.* This body of popular and scholarly works about White House history has been read and enjoyed by millions of Americans.

Since the White House Historical Association's founding, its publications and educational programs have expanded dramatically, and we continue, as ever, to pursue our mission to preserve the White House and to acquire and conserve its furnishings. It has been a privilege to be a part of the association throughout its first 40 years and to contribute to its mission of bringing to the public the history of a house and a national symbol that reflect the life of America.

Robert L. Breeden
Chairman of the Board of Directors
White House Historical Association
1990–2000

Robert L. Breeden

Introduction

We all rightly claim a bit of the White House. After all, the mythical Uncle Sam lives there. It has been the stage on which our presidents have performed both in crisis and in tranquillity and also the headquarters for launching the great national programs and goals that have shaped America for more than two centuries.

So it was fitting that when the White House turned 200 the White House Historical Association should celebrate. With the enthusiastic support of President and Mrs. William J. Clinton, we had candles and cake, champagne, and many toasts. Hundreds of guests dined, and thousands of old stories were told about the grand old structure. We had even more: the U.S. Postal Service issued a commemorative stamp, the U.S. Mint forged a special medallion, and artist Jamie Wyeth painted a birthday portrait, *Dawn • The White House • 2000.* John Adams (portrayed by an actor) rode to the back door in a horse-drawn carriage at noon on November 1, 2000, almost exactly two centuries after his first arrival. This time President Clinton and David McCullough were on hand to talk about how it must have been, and what has happened since. Drums rolled and fifes played. The White House basked in the autumn sun and the great history of its past.

The White House is the most famous and important building in the world. Historians suggest that it is as well known a symbol of freedom in all parts of the globe as the Statue of Liberty and the Stars and Stripes. The White House is more than sandstone and mortar: it is part of the American spirit; it is a repository of the nation's memory. The White House embodies the meaning of the republic. Say "the

White House" and the phrase catches every heart. Sometimes the building seems almost alive, particularly in times of tragedy and triumph. The familiar facade offered comfort to thousands who gathered on the lawn after the devastating attack on Pearl Harbor, and thousands swarmed around the White House when the great war finally ended in triumph for the United States and its allies.

Every president who has lived there has at some time or another testified how moved he was while walking through White House corridors, so rich with history and in later years lined with the portraits of those who preceded him. Each has left his special mark.

Our 200th birthday party was marked by one of the most memorable dinners ever given at the White House. On November 9, 2000, former President Gerald R. Ford and Mrs. Ford, President Jimmy Carter and Mrs. Carter, and President George Bush and Mrs. Bush were guests of President and Mrs. William J. Clinton. Lady Bird Johnson, widow of President Lyndon B. Johnson, attended, and a special tribute was made to President Ronald Reagan and Mrs. Reagan, who were unable to attend. The former presidents were drawn back to the White House despite the fact that the national election two days before had not been resolved. In fact, the evening was on that account even more meaningful, showing the world that despite American political differences the contending party leaders could come together to demonstrate the underlying unity of this democratic society.

The presidents toasted the great history of the White House and its meaning in these times. Each spoke of how he had been influenced by the White House aura, which was a creation of the events and personalities of two centuries of living and working in the same building. Then in the foyer of the White House, the guests listened to one more tribute, this one from the Marine Band, "the President's Own," so named by Thomas Jefferson. The anniversary piece was called "The President's House: A Bicentennial Tribute."

The final act of this special birthday was a three-day symposium. Scholars gathered to read papers and discuss the nature of the men and women who had lived in the White House and the inner dynamics of the institution of the presidency and the families caught up in the exercise of great power. More than 300 historians, teachers, and other interested people listened and mingled and saw the White House on a special tour hosted by Chief Usher Gary Walters, Curator Betty Monkman, and the White House's curatorial staff.

The celebration of the 200th anniversary of the White House was such a success and brought response from people around the world because so much of it was televised. We felt it worthwhile to publish this small book of tribute, which creates a record of one of the most memorable birthday parties in our nation's history.

Hugh S. Sidey
President of the Board of Directors
White House Historical Association
1998–2001

John Adams

On November 1, 2000, two hundred years to the day after President John Adams arrived at the south entrance of the White House in his coach, President William J. Clinton marked the event for the nation by presiding over a reenactment that welcomed Adams to the President's House. Historian David McCullough gave life to those early days at the President's House, and President Clinton spoke of the enduring symbolism that transcends the building's roles of home and office.

President John Adams (portrayed by Steven Perlman) arrives by carriage at the south front of the White House. President Clinton and guests witness the event from the South Portico.

Front View of the Presidents House in the City of Washington.

The earliest published view of the White House, from an English travel book of 1807.

November 1, 1800

MR. DAVID MCCULLOUGH

Mr. President, distinguished guests, ladies and gentlemen. The first president to move into what was then known as the President's House, John Adams, of Quincy, Massachusetts, arrived here at this entrance at midday, Saturday, November 1, 1800, at just about this time. Very little looked as we now see it. The new Federal City of Washington was no city at all. The Capitol was only half finished. Except for a few nondescript stores and hotels in the vicinity of the Capitol, the rest was mostly tree stumps and swamp.

The house itself was still quite unfinished. Fires had to be kept burning in all the fireplaces to help dry the wet plaster. Only a few rooms were ready. Only one twisting back stairway connected the floors. Though the president's furniture had arrived, shipped from Philadelphia, it looked lost in these enormous rooms. The only picture hanging was Gilbert Stuart's full-length portrait of George Washington, which still hangs in the East Room.

These beautiful grounds did not exist. It was a different setting; it was a different country; and it was a different time. In that age no one ever knew when anyone was going to arrive anywhere, for certain, including the president of the United States. So on that historic morning, two district commissioners were inside inspecting the work when they happened to look out the window and comment, "There is the president of the United States." He had just rolled up in his carriage.

John Adams was the first head of state to occupy the White House. Portrait (detail) by John Trumbull, c. 1792–93.

*The President's House
is seen in the distance in
this 1801 watercolor by
J. Benford. The building on
the far right is Blodget's
Hotel, which resembled the
White House and was also
built by James Hoban.*

With the president were his secretary, Billy Shaw, and one servant on horseback, John Briesler, who became the first steward for the White House. There was nobody else: no honor guard, no band playing, no entourage of any kind. But who was that man who walked through these doors, the first of 40 presidents who have lived here thus far?

John Adams had just celebrated his 61st birthday two days before, en route from Philadelphia. He was about 5 feet 7 inches, which was midsize in that day, and stout, but physically very strong. He stood erect, shoulders back. He was accustomed at home to building stone walls and bringing in the hay. He was a farmer's son, descended from four generations of plain, God-fearing New England farmers, and proud of it. He was, of course, one of our Founding Fathers, a leading figure in the American Revolution. Thomas Jefferson called him "the Colossus of Independence" for the part he played in driving the Declaration of Independence through the Continental Congress in that fateful summer of 1776. His role was decisive.

On missions to Europe in the midst of war, John Adams traveled farther and under more adverse conditions in the service of his country than any American of his time. It was he who secured the desperately needed loans from the Dutch to help finance the war. He was a signer of the Paris Peace Treaty that ended the war and the first American to appear before King George III as a minister for the new United States of America. Between times he also drafted the oldest written constitution still in use in the world today—the Constitution of the Commonwealth of Massachusetts, written 10 years before our own Constitution, which it greatly influenced. He was our first vice president, under George Washington, and was elected president in 1796, defeating his old friend Thomas Jefferson.

The President's House in December 1800 as envisioned by artist Tom Freeman (2000). John Adams used the south front as the main entrance to the unfinished house. Visitors entered the oval room, known today as the Blue Room, from a temporary wooden balcony accessed by long stairs. The tall South Portico was not added until 1824.

John Adams could be proud, vain, irritable, short-tempered. He was also brilliant, warmhearted, humorous, a devoted husband and father, and a lifelong talker, an all-out, full-time talker. He loved Don Quixote. He loved the English poets. He carried a book with him everywhere he traveled and once said to his son, John Quincy, "You'll never be alone with a poet in your pocket." He never had any money to speak of, and he is the only one of our Founding Fathers who, as a matter of principle, never owned a slave.

Further, John Adams had the immense good fortune to be married to Abigail Smith Adams, one of the most extraordinary Americans of that extraordinary era. And their letters to one another constitute a national treasure. They number well over a thousand.

John Adams was a great man and a highly principled president in tumultuous times. Though gravely mistaken when he signed the infamous Alien and Sedition Acts, he had the good sense and determination and the courage to keep America from going to war with France, which was a very great accomplishment indeed, with far-reaching consequences. But let us not forget, too, that it was John Adams who nominated George Washington to be commander in chief of the Continental Army. It was John Adams who insisted that Jefferson be the one to write the Declaration of Independence. And it was President John Adams who made John Marshall chief justice of the Supreme Court. As a casting director alone, he was brilliant.

Abigail Adams did not arrive here to join her husband until two weeks later, in that long-ago November. She could never get over the size of the house. She called it "the castle" and hung her laundry to dry in the then unfinished East Room. The Adamses lived in the house less than four months, and it was not a happy time for them. Adams learned of his defeat for reelection by Jefferson in what was, perhaps, the most vicious presidential campaign in our history. Then, within days, he and Abigail received word—devastating word—that their second son, Charles, had died in New York of alcoholism.

There were men and women in that day, in their time, who would have refused to live in the White House in the condition it was in. But the Adamses made do without complaint. On January 1, 1801, they held the first New Year's Day reception here ever— an open house.

On his first evening in this house, following a light supper, John Adams retired

Before I end my Letter I pray Heaven to bestow the best of Blessings on this House and all that shall hereafter inhabit it. May none but honest and wise Men ever rule under this roof.

I Shall not attempt a description of it. You will form the best Idea of it from Inspection.

Mr Brisler is very anxious for the arrival of the Man and Women, and I am much more so for that of the Ladies. I am with unabated Confidence and affection your

John Adams

Mrs Adams

early for the night. We may picture him with a single candle climbing that twisting back stairway. Early the next morning he went to his desk on the second floor and addressed a now-famous letter to Abigail. Franklin Roosevelt thought so highly of the letter, and of two sentences in it, that he had them carved into the mantelpiece

The first letter written by John Adams from the White House (left) to his wife Abigail includes the famous phrase that is inscribed in the State Dining Room mantel (above).

in the State Dining Room. And when Harry Truman supervised the rebuilding of the White House, he insisted that that inscription remain where it is today. When John F. Kennedy was president, he had the inscription carved into the mantelpiece in marble. "I pray heaven," Adams wrote, "to bestow the best of blessings on this house and all that shall hereafter inhabit it. May none but honest and wise men ever rule under this roof."

John Adams lived another 25 years, to age 90, longer than any president. As it happened, he and Thomas Jefferson died on the same day. And it wasn't just any day; it

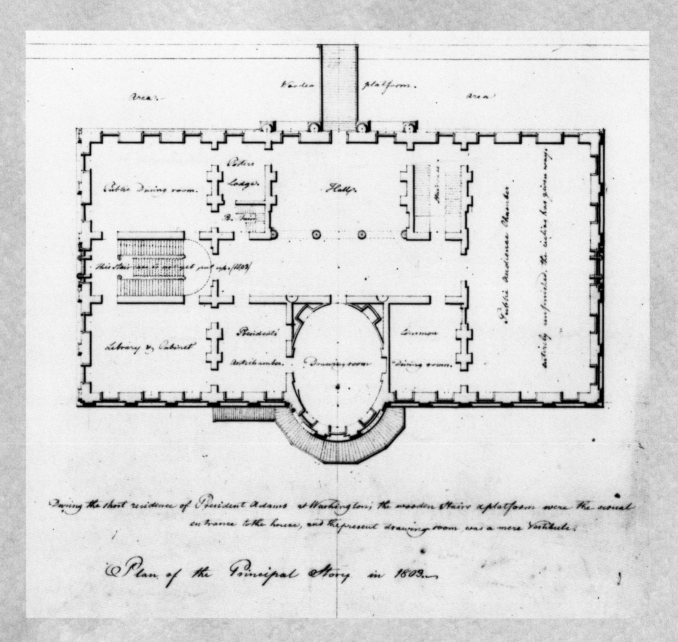

Plan of the Principal Story in 1803

Benjamin H. Latrobe's 1807 drawing of the state floor of the President's House with the rooms designated as President Thomas Jefferson used them in 1803.

In his notes, Latrobe described the wooden exterior stair built by President Adams and stated that the oval "Drawing room" was used as an entrance vestibule.

The Adamses used what is labeled as a "Library & Cabinet" as a levee or reception room, the "President's antichamber" as a family dining room, and the "Common Dining room" as a bedroom.

Only the service stairs were built by 1800. The drawing is an early and accurate depiction of the original use and condition of the White House.

Historian David McCullough speaks on the Adams White House. President William J. Clinton and National Park Service Director Robert Stanton join McCullough on the Blue Room porch.

was *the* day—July 4, 1826—the 50th anniversary of the signing of the Declaration of Independence. A few days before Adams's death, a delegation of his Quincy neighbors came to call on him. The old president sat in an armchair in his library as they asked if he could give them a toast that they might read aloud at the town's Fourth of July celebration. "I will give you," said Adams, "Independence Forever." Asked if he would like to add something more to that, he said, "Not a word."

That was the man who first occupied the White House. I think how pleased he and Abigail would be if they were here to see how we've gathered today, to see the country they so loved still independent, still united and thriving, still strong, still free, and this grand old house looking so magnificent. But then, maybe they are here with us today.

My Dear Child,

I arrived here on Sunday last, without meeting any accident worth noticing, except losing ourselves when we left Baltimore, and going eight or nine miles on the Frederick road, by which means we were obliged to go the other eight through woods…woods are all you see, from Baltimore until you reach the city, which is only so in name.… In the city there are buildings enough, if they were compact and finished, to accommodate Congress and those attached to it; but as they are, and scattered as they are, I see no great comfort in them.…The {President's} house is upon a grand and superb scale, requiring thirty servants to attend and keep the apartments in proper order.… To assist us in this great castle, and render less attendance necessary, bells are wholly wanting, not one single one being hung through the whole house, and promises are all you can obtain. This is so great an inconvenience, that I know not what to do, or how to do.… if they will put me up some bells, and let me have wood enough to keep fires, I design to be pleased. I could content myself almost anywhere three months; but, surrounded with forests, can you believe that wood is not to be had, because people cannot be found to cut and cart it!…We have, indeed, come into a new country. You must keep all this to yourself, and, when asked how I like it, say that I write you the situation is beautiful, which is true. The house is made habitable, but there is not a single apartment finished… and the great unfinished audience-room I make a drying-room of, to hang up the clothes in.… Up stairs there is the oval room, which is designed for the drawing room, and has the crimson furniture in it. It is a very handsome room now; but, when completed, it will be beautiful. If the twelve years, in which this place has been considered as the future seat of government, had been improved, as they would have been if in New England, very many of the present inconveniences would have been removed. It is a beautiful spot, capable of every improvement, and, the more I view it, the more I am delighted with it.

Abigail Adams —

North front of the President's House, c. 1800. Washington merchant, entrepreneur, and amateur artist Samuel Blodget Jr. rendered this faithful representation of the President's House. The entablature's carved laurel branches were an artistic enhancement as the plaque was actually blank.

President's House

President's House

In the Presidency of Jefferson

Sketch of the North Front   196 Feet

The United States Army Old Guard Fife & Drum Corps precede the arrival of John Adams. President Clinton's special guests include Adams family descendants, Representatives William Delahunt and Edward Markey from Massachusetts, Washington, D.C., Mayor Anthony Williams, and board members of the White House Historical Association.

After the arrival ceremony, guests enjoy a reception in the Blue Room. Members of the Adams family pose with President Clinton before the portrait of John Adams.

David McCullough chats with President Clinton as Chelsea Clinton and guests join them in the Red Room.

PRESIDENT CLINTON

Thank you very much, and good afternoon. I know I speak for all of us in thanking
David McCullough for that wonderful review of President Adams's life and presidency.
We could all listen to him all day and never stop learning. I thank Bob Stanton for his
distinguished work at the National Park Service. I'd like to thank Representatives
William Delahunt and Edward Markey for coming here, for representing the state of
Massachusetts, home of the Adams family. I thank all the descendants of the Adams
family who are here with us today, and I know that they share in the pride all Americans
feel for the contributions of John Adams and his son, John Quincy Adams, and so many
other members of their family, to the richness of our nation's history. Mayor Anthony
Williams, thank you for joining us here today. I'd like to thank the members of the
White House Historical Association board, including Bob Breeden and Hugh Sidey and
Neil Horstman, who helped make this month of celebrations possible. I'd like to thank
the people here at the White House who played their role—Melanne Verveer, assistant
to the president and chief of staff to the first lady, who has worked so hard on the historic
preservation work we've been honored to do these last eight years; and especially our
chief usher, Gary Walters, and through him all the members of the White House staff.
For 200 years now they have been the unsung heroes, making this place work every
day, making it a place available to the American people and still a home for the
president and his family. I'd also like to thank the United States Marine Band.
For more than 200 years they have set a standard of musical excellence that has

Hugh Sidey, president of the White House Historical Association (left), and David McCullough (right) pose with President John Adams (portrayed by Steven Perlman).

During the reception following the arrival ceremony, President Clinton greets David McCullough's family.

enriched this house and our entire nation. They have been "the President's Own,"
and for me it has been a special honor and treat. They have stirred the spirits of more
people than President Adams could ever have imagined when he signed the bill creating
the Marine Band. And today their music is in honor of his memory. So let's give them
a big hand. Thank you very much for being here.

As David McCullough just said, the capital city President Adams helped to
shape was a very different place from the Washington we know today. Our nation was
new and still carving out the symbols that would define it forever. History tells us that
even as the city's planners debated the final design of this house, masons laid its stone
foundations more than 4 feet thick. Like our nation's Founders, these men were building
a monument to freedom, and they wanted it to last. In 1814, when the British troops
captured Washington, they entered the President's House, as it was then known, to find
supper still on the table. The first lady, Dolley Madison, had prepared it for her husband
but had to leave it behind when she fled. Well, the British were uncouth enough to
eat the supper before they set fire to the house. When the smoke finally cleared, it was
just a charred shell; but the stone walls stood strong, and so did our nation.

For two centuries now, Americans have looked to the White House as a symbol
of leadership in times of crisis, of reassurance in times of uncertainty, of continuity in
times of change, of celebration in times of joy. These walls carry the story of America.
It was here at the White House that President Jefferson first unrolled maps of a
bountiful continent to plan the Lewis and Clark expedition; here that President Lincoln
signed the Emancipation Proclamation freeing the slaves, some of whose ancestors had

quarried the very stone from which the White House was built; here that President Roosevelt held the fireside chats, willing his nation through the Depression, then marshaling our allies through the war.

Over the course of two centuries, the White House has also been home to 40 presidents and their families, including mine. Hillary, Chelsea, and I love this house. We have loved living here. It is still a thrill every time I drive up in a car or land on the back lawn in the helicopter, just to look at this magnificent place and to feel the honor of sharing its history for these eight years. We are profoundly grateful to the American people for letting it be our home for these years. One of the best things about it, like any home, is welcoming others to share in its beauty and history, not just heads of state or great artists or famous scholars, but the people this house really belongs to—the American people.

The White House is the only executive residence in the entire world that is regularly open, free of charge, to the public. And every year, nearly a million and a half people walk through its halls, marveling at the history and taking away perhaps a little better sense of who we are as a nation. Hillary has taken a special interest in supporting this living museum, showcasing the full diversity of our nation's art, culture, and history. I thank her, especially, for establishing the sculpture garden over here to my left in the Jacqueline Kennedy Garden. And from the day we moved in, she has also devoted herself to preserving the White House and has personally overseen the restoration of several of its public rooms, rooms on the residence floor, on the second floor, and on the third floor. Working with the

White House Historical Association, she's also helped to raise a lasting endowment, something that is profoundly important because it will enable us to better preserve the White House and its collections for all generations to come.

In renewing this beloved monument to our nation's history and freedom, we also renew our commitment to the dream of our Founders—that our democracy, built upon bedrocks of liberty and justice, will grow ever stronger and remain forever young. So as the White House enters its third century, let us remember President John Adams, being grateful to him for his many contributions to our republic and his determination to define us as one nation. And let us share his prayer that in this house the best of blessings will be bestowed and that leaders here will find the wisdom and the guidance to do well by our nation, to do well by all of our people, and to be responsible leaders in the larger world. That's what John Adams tried to do; that's what America has tried to do for 200 years now. We are still in the business of forming that more perfect union of our Founders' dreams. I hope and believe John Adams would be pleased.

The White House

1800–2000 ANNIVERSARY

2000

The President and Mrs. Clinton
request the pleasure of the company of
Mr. and Mrs. Downs
at a dinner to celebrate
The Two hundredth Anniversary
of The White House
on Thursday, November 9, 2000
at seven-thirty o'clock

Black Tie

East Entrance

Anniversary Dinner

Just two days after a national election, so close it failed to determine a president-elect, a spectacular event was held in the East Room at the White House. Political partisanship was put aside on this evening to celebrate the 200th anniversary of the Executive Mansion as the home and office of the chief executive. President and Mrs. Clinton welcomed Lady Bird Johnson, Gerald and Betty Ford, Jimmy and Rosalynn Carter, and George and Barbara Bush, as well as 200 additional guests to mark the occasion. The guests of honor sat together at a head table and were served dinner on a new state service donated by the White House Historical Association to commemorate the anniversary. The menu, researched to recall the regional cuisine of 200 years ago, included a duck consommé, striped bass, smoked lamb, salad and cheese, and a floating island—a favorite dessert of President and Mrs. John Adams. President Clinton underscored the importance of the event by noting, "Never before have this many presidents and first ladies gathered in this great room." After dinner, Presidents Ford, Carter, Bush, and Clinton, eyewitnesses of the recent past, spoke of the inspiration and legacy of the historic White House. The evening was concluded by a special performance of "The President's House: A Bicentennial Tribute" by the United States Marine Band in the Entrance Hall, where they have played music for state functions since 1801. It was a remarkable evening without precedent, including speeches that will resonate down through the ages.

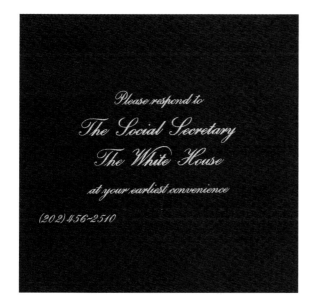

*The anniversary
dinner invitation.*

Please respond to
The Social Secretary
The White House
at your earliest convenience

(202) 456-2510

Reception

Prior to the 200th anniversary dinner, President and
Mrs. William J. Clinton hosted a reception in the second floor
family quarters. The presidents and first ladies gathered in the
Center Hall where they signed a limited a number of *giclées*
of the commemorative painting *Dawn • The White House • 2000*,
by Jamie Wyeth. The dinner guests were given reproductions
of the painting.

Left:
The Center Hall of the
second floor family quarters.

Right:
Social Secretary Capricia
Marshall reviews the evening
scenario with the presidents
and first ladies.

Overleaf:
Presidents and first ladies
proceed to dinner under the
watchful eye of President
Reagan.

Dinner

Following the reception the President and Mrs. Clinton escorted Mrs. Johnson, President and Mrs. Ford, President and Mrs. Carter, and President and Mrs. Bush to the State Dining Room for an official photograph. The President and Mrs. Clinton and the former presidents and first ladies then proceeded to the East Room for dinner.

Mr. Robert Breeden, chairman of the board of the White House Historical Association, opened the evening's festivities.

*President and Mrs. Clinton
escort Mrs. Johnson to dinner.*

Robert L. Breeden,
chairman of the Board
of Directors, White House
Historical Association,
1990–2000.

MR. ROBERT BREEDEN

President and Mrs. Clinton, Mrs. Johnson, President
and Mrs. Ford, President and Mrs. Carter, President
and Mrs. Bush, and honored guests, good evening.

Before I make the presentation of special gifts to the White House on behalf of the
White House Historical Association, I would like for a moment to take us back to this room 200
years ago when President John Adams became the first resident on November 1. The room was
completely unfurnished, with raw brick walls; wood shavings and carpenter tools littered the floor.
Later, after Mrs. Adams joined the president on November 16, she used this vast, empty room to
dry the presidential laundry. With no e-mail, television, or telephone, no one knew exactly when
the president would arrive. His coach brought him almost unnoticed down a dirt Pennsylvania
Avenue. No fifes and drums, no parade, no cheering crowds. Mrs. William Thornton noted in her
diary that day that she had seen the president and his secretary pass by. At about 1 o'clock in the
afternoon he entered a house smelling of wood fires built to dry the freshly plastered walls and
wallpaper paste made with flour, water—and beer; the beer was used as a binder. After nightfall,
President Adams walked with a single candle up the servants' stairs—the only stairs finished
at the time—to his second floor bedroom.

From his office next to his bedroom, President Adams conducted the business of state.
That didn't involve more than communicating across the way to two brick buildings that housed
the entire executive branch, with a total of some 130 employees. These workers and most of the
populace were scurrying about as the government moved from Philadelphia to the new capital city.

Adams once said that he would just as soon live in a row house somewhere in the city as in the new mansion. Fortunately, he changed his mind and started a tradition followed by every president since.

Tonight we commemorate Adams's residency and that tradition. In honor of the occasion the White House Historical Association is pleased to present to the White House a pair of elegant French porcelain vases made about 1820. One has the portrait of President Washington; the other has a portrait of President Adams, the first occupant.

The association is also pleased to present a mahogany desk and bookcase, circa 1830, for the Red Room, and the Clinton state dinner and dessert service with designs inspired by White House architectural motifs. The china is being used for the first time at tonight's dinner.

To commemorate this anniversary, the association commissioned a painting by Jamie Wyeth, entitled Dawn • The White House • 2000. *The painting is here on display tonight. Jamie, would you please rise? Thank you so much. The association especially wants to thank MBNA Foundation for underwriting the painting, which is on loan to the White House. Artist's proofs of the painting were given to President Clinton, the former presidents, and Mrs. Johnson earlier this evening, and they signed each other's proofs to mark the occasion.*

As a memento of this historic celebration, Mrs. Clinton and the former first ladies have received a copy of our new book, The White House: Its Historic Furnishings and First Families. *The books have been signed by the author, White House curator Betty Monkman, and include forewords by each of the first ladies. The association is most grateful to the family of Ambassador Walter H. Annenberg, who so generously established the Hon. Walter H. Annenberg White House Publications Fund that made the book possible.*

Let me add our sincere thanks to the United States Postal Service for creating a commemorative White House postage stamp and to the United States Mint for producing a

White House medallion in honor of the anniversary.

    These are only a few of the activities and events the association is sponsoring this year.
One person has worked tirelessly to make them happen, and I would like to ask him to rise and be
recognized—the association's president, familiar to all of us—Hugh Sidey. Thank you, Hugh.

    To paraphrase John Adams's prayer written on his second day in the White House,
"Let us pray heaven to bestow the best of blessings on this great old house."

    Thank you very much.

PRESIDENT CLINTON

"Never before have this
many presidents and first
ladies gathered in this
great room."
—William J. Clinton

Good evening, Mrs. Johnson, President and Mrs. Ford, President and Mrs. Carter, President and Mrs. Bush, distinguished guests. It has been said that an invitation to dinner at the White House is one of the highest compliments a president can bestow on anyone. Tonight Hillary and I would amend that to say that an even higher compliment has been bestowed on us by your distinguished presence this evening. In the entire 200 years of the White House's history, never before have this many presidents and first ladies gathered in this great room.

    Hillary and I are grateful beyond words to have served as temporary stewards of the people's house these last eight years, an honor exceeded only by the privilege of service that comes with a key to the front door. In a short span of 200 years, those whom the wings of history have brought to this place have shaped not only their own times but have also left behind a living legacy for our own. In ways both large and small, each and every one of you has cast your light upon this house, and has left it and our country brighter for it. For that, Hillary and I—and all Americans—owe you a great debt of gratitude. I salute you and all those yet to grace these halls with the words of the very first occupant of the White House, John Adams, who said, "I pray heaven to bestow the best of blessings on this house and all that shall hereafter inhabit it. May none but the honest and wise rule under this roof."

Ladies and gentlemen, I ask you to join me in a toast to Mrs. Johnson, President and Mrs. Ford, President and Mrs. Carter, and President and Mrs. Bush for their honest and wise service to the people while they inhabited this house.

MRS. CLINTON

President and Mrs. Ford, President and Mrs. Carter, President and Mrs. Bush, and Lady Bird Johnson, as well as members of the families of other presidents who have joined us here this evening, we thank you all for your tireless commitment to making this house flourish in all of its roles: as the home of the first family, as a symbol of democracy, and as a living museum open to all of our citizens. I also want to thank Bob Breeden, Hugh Sidey, and Neil Horstman for making this extraordinary celebration possible. We've already heard from Bob what it must have been like for John and Abigail Adams when they first arrived here 200 years ago this month. It is astonishing as we look around this absolutely glorious East Room to think about Mrs. Adams hanging her wash.

As some of you know, Gilbert Stuart's portrait of George Washington hangs in this room, and it inspires my favorite story about the history of the house. One of my predecessors during the War of 1812, Dolley Madison, actually saved this extraordinary painting when she received word from her husband that the British were on their way to Washington, and he ordered her to flee. Like any sensible woman she took that into account but decided instead to stay until she had saved many of the most valuable items of what was then a very limited White House collection. It wasn't the account books or her personal possessions but rather some of the items that represented the founding of our republic. She was the most remarkable woman. Here the British are marching on Washington, her husband has ordered her to leave, and everyone is scurrying around, and she takes time to write a letter to her sister: "Our kind friend, Mr. Carroll, has come to hasten my departure, and is in a very bad humor with me because I insist on waiting until the large picture of Gen. Washington is secured, and it requires to be unscrewed from the wall. This process was found too tedious for these perilous moments. I have ordered the frame to be broken, and the canvas taken out—it is done, and the precious portrait placed in the hands of two gentlemen of New York, for safekeeping. And now dear sister I must leave this house...."

I have been reminded on several occasions by the British ambassador that when the British did break through the lines and they arrived here they found the meal that Mrs. Madison had prepared for her husband and his officers, which they sat down and ate before burning the house to the ground. And she was in a long line of those of us privileged to be temporary residents here, to understand that we are all stewards of this house. It certainly has been the privilege of a lifetime for our family to live here and to have a chance to help preserve its history and then share it with people.

Just today I received a letter from the American Association of Museums letting us know that they have recently voted again to award accreditation to the White House, the highest distinction a museum can receive. It is a testimony to the many people since the Adamses moved in who have worked to protect the history, arts, culture, ideas, and

"Now I am sure that when the White House celebrates its 300th anniversary they will do a reenactment ceremony highlighting our quaint methods of transportation, the old-fashioned ways we used to communicate such as e-mail and fax, but more than anything they, too, will look back and give thanks to all of our leaders who have helped to preserve this venerable house."
—*Hillary Rodham Clinton*

innovations of this living museum—and many of those who have made these contributions are with us this evening. Now I am sure that when the White House celebrates its 300th anniversary they will do a reenactment ceremony highlighting our quaint methods of transportation, the old-fashioned ways we used to communicate such as e-mail and fax, but more than anything they, too, will look back and give thanks to all of our leaders who have helped to preserve this venerable house. And they will give thanks to all of the first families, many of whom are with us in representative capacity and the others, sadly, like the Reagans, who could not be here. They will also give thanks to the White House Historical Association and the Committee for the Preservation of the White House. They will give thanks to Gary Walters and the entire Executive Residence staff and the curators who have worked here. They will give thanks to the many artists who have entertained us, inspired us, and reminded us of who we are as a nation and who we want to become. And they will give thanks to many of you in this room who have given very special gifts to the White House collection that will be part of its history, and to the historians who have made sure that Americans learn the history of this house and pass it on to their children.

It is now my great honor to introduce someone who has taught us about the American presidency for almost half a century. He covered nine presidents and traveled the world shedding light on the great events of our time. Today as the president of the White House Historical Association, Hugh Sidey continues working tirelessly to teach all of our citizens, old and young alike, about the White House, its culture, its history, and its meaning to our democracy. It is my honor to introduce Hugh Sidey.

Hugh S. Sidey, president of the Board of Directors, White House Historical Association, 1998–2001.

MR. HUGH SIDEY

This is such a magnificent night. It will be at least 12 hours before I come back to earth! Thank you so much, Mrs. Clinton. I'm going to stand history on its head tonight by suggesting that there is more talent gathered under this roof than when Thomas Jefferson dined here alone.

You know, earlier in the day and yesterday it was suggested, or at least people said, "Well, are you going to go ahead with this? In this time?" I said, "Absolutely, more than ever." And so did everybody else.

This is the 200th anniversary of a building, but all of us know tonight that it is more than that. The White House is a meaning; it is a spirit. It is a whole two centuries of history. It is the heartbeat of this country, and tonight we celebrate that just as much as we celebrate these wonderful walls. I'm sure we all feel that—the Clintons our hosts, and all the presidents and first ladies, and all of you who take pride and joy in this building, as we do as well, and those of you in America who may be watching, too. We all feel this spirit that we come together no matter what our arguments or our irritations are, and we march on, as we are tonight. And it's a glorious moment, really, in our history.

Now let the people who have lived here talk to you a little about it. And before that I want to have somebody very special rise, Lady Bird Johnson, who represents, of course, her husband. Would you rise, Lady Bird?

And there is a living president who, of course, could not be here, Ronald Reagan. And perhaps his wife is watching, and they will get a little touch of this. So I would like just a little tribute, one more from the East Room to the Gipper.

"I was probably saying 'Hurry up Lyndon,'" recalled Mrs. Johnson as she spoke of this image of her with President Johnson eating breakfast on Inauguration Day, January 20, 1965.

President Ronald Reagan and First Lady Nancy Reagan are happily greeted by Rex, their Cavalier King Charles spaniel, as they exit from Marine One upon returning to the White House.

And the first one we would like to hear from is President Gerald Ford. He had no idea, in the years ahead, that he would be president, nor did we have any idea that he would be president, but Gerald Ford came in and he did end our long national nightmare. And he did it with grace, and he did it with dignity. And he is here tonight to talk a little bit about his time in the White House. And I have one more fondness of him—he has shown that a person can rise to the top without all that hair that others have. Mr. Ford.

PRESIDENT FORD

Thank you, Hugh, for that generous introduction. Someone asked me on the way over this evening if I was glad to be back at the White House. I told him that in the wake of my recent visit to the hospital, and with all due respect to W. C. Fields, I'd rather be anywhere than Philadelphia.

Betty and I want to thank you, Mr. President and Mrs. Clinton, along with the White House Historical Association, for welcoming back some former tenants of America's most distinguished public housing. As you know, ours is an exclusive trade union—yet we look forward to welcoming you as its newest member come January 20. Take it from one who knows all about losing a close presidential election, there is life after Inauguration Day, with new and unexpected joys. Certainly few observers in January 1977 would have predicted that Jimmy and I would become the closest of friends. Yet we have, bonded by our years in this office, and this house.

Accident or not, I think the timing of our reunion is providential. Once again, the world's oldest republic has demonstrated the youthful vitality of its institutions—and the ability to come together after a hard-fought campaign. The clash of partisan political ideas remains just that, to be quickly followed by a peaceful transfer of authority. It's a far cry from 200 years ago, when John Adams was so miffed over his defeat that he refused to attend Thomas Jefferson's inauguration. As it happens, this week's celebration coincides with the anniversary of Abigail Adams's arrival in the nation's new capital. History records that Abigail was a much better politician than John.

Back then, first ladies weren't supposed to involve themselves in anything so demeaning as the political arena. Critics in the press took to labeling Abigail Adams "Mrs. President"—and they didn't mean it to be flattering. A lot has changed since then, most of it for the better. I know whereof I speak. Wherever I went during the 1976 campaign I ran into people wearing buttons that read, "Betty's Husband for President."

Betty and I, of course, occupy a unique place in the White House fraternity. We're the only residents of 1600 Pennsylvania Avenue who never wanted to live here. As Jimmy and Rosalynn can attest, by the autumn of 1976, we were as reluctant to leave as we had been to come in the first place.

Two centuries have passed since John Adams uttered his famous prayer for all those who would live under this roof. Anyone who experienced the tumultuous events of August 1974 will appreciate my own prayer—that no future American president is ever called to this office as I was—and that our Constitution is never again put to such a test. Those were surreal times.

For six days after my East Room inaugural, the Fords continued living in our Alexandria home while the White House underwent a transition of its own. Back on the home front our daughter, Susan, announced that she had no intention of abandoning blue

jeans just because she was going to live at the White House. Betty chimed in, declaring that while she was willing to make the move, she was too old to change and that she could only be herself—whether living on Pennsylvania Avenue or on Crown View Drive in Alexandria. Why do you think I made my own English muffins!

Yet as the days went by and we reached out to my old friends on Capitol Hill, welcoming the Black Caucus, George Meany, and others who for too long had felt excluded from this place, I was struck by America's amazing capacity for self-healing. And not a day passed that the devotion and professionalism of the White House staff didn't impress me.

I have often been asked if I ever saw ghosts in the White House. The answer is no —unless you count the last week of the '76 campaign, when I saw the ghost of a chance! Nevertheless, I was constantly humbled by the inescapable presence of my predecessors— by Jackson and Lincoln and the two Roosevelts and Truman and Eisenhower and so many others who live on in our imagination and our idealism. I think, too, of the first ladies, those unsung heroines of American democracy—unelected, unpaid, all too often unfairly criticized for their clothes, their decor, or their children. Each provided unceasing love and support not only to her husband and family but to the country she also served.

For more than a few of these families, this has been a house of sorrow: a child dies, a spouse falls ill, elections are lost, reputations suffer. Certainly the Fords of Grand Rapids had our ups and downs. There was Betty's bout with breast cancer, which fortunately led millions of American women to be more vigilant about their own health. There was the aftermath of Watergate and the cruel days of April 1975, when Americans left Indochina and we worked frantically to rescue thousands of Vietnamese refugees. But there was also America's Bicentennial, when this very room witnessed glittering events at which the rest of

Susan Ford focuses on her father, President Gerald R. Ford, at his desk in the Oval Office as he reviews examples of her photographs.

the world acknowledged the abiding strength of our freedoms.

On the stage of American history the White House has played many roles. It is, among other things, an office building, a museum, a television studio, a cultural showcase, a think tank, a war room, and, from time to time, unofficially, a campaign headquarters. It is a universally recognized symbol of our democracy. Most of all, however, it is a home. Betty and I will never forget the evening in July 1976, when the elevator carrying Queen Elizabeth, Prince Philip, and their hosts to the private quarters opened to reveal one of our sons decidedly underdressed and hunting for his shirt studs for a white tie state dinner. "Don't worry," Her Majesty told us. "I have one at home just like him."

But even that was nothing compared to the dinner which followed. No sooner had I invited Her Majesty to join me on the dance floor than the Marine Band broke into a spirited rendition of "The Lady Is a Tramp." Only narrowly did we avert an international incident—not to mention a court martial.

Nearly 80 years ago, President Coolidge stood outside the White House as a friend mischievously asked him, "I wonder who lives there?" "No one," said Coolidge. "They just come and go." Tonight, I wish to pay tribute to the people who don't come and go: to the curators who care for a nation's priceless heritage, to the doormen and butlers and cooks, the housemaids and ushers and gardeners—to everyone who aids, comforts, and inspires a president and his loved ones. So with your permission, Mr. President, I would like to propose a toast: from our families to the White House family, for all you do to make this old house a home. God bless you all.

MR. HUGH SIDEY

Thank you, President Ford. And now a little bit from President Carter. He came in with rare candor and direct talk. This city wasn't really ready for that, as you know, but something happened in that time, and Jimmy Carter's presidency has gone on and on, and today he has a remarkable following and a remarkable reputation and a presence in this world that has carried all through the years and into this world now.

All of us in this room, I think, have memories of the White House at certain times. I well remember coming back from Dallas and standing under those elms as they brought the shattered body of John Kennedy back. But then there was a great moment, too. That's when President Carter came down from Camp David with the Camp David Accords—one more tortuous step for peace. We gathered on the

lawn. And the old adversaries and the others involved gathered on the front lawn of the White House. It was a sunny day, and I remember the bells of Saint John's Church began to chime, and you looked up at that scene and the White House was in back, and it was almost as if that old building had its arms around those peacemakers. Mr. Carter.

PRESIDENT CARTER

Hearing President Gerald Ford's comments tonight, I recall the ferocious political campaign he waged from the White House in the summer of 1976. I also remember the first sentence of my Inaugural Address a few months later, when I said, "For myself and for our Nation, I want to thank my predecessor for all he has done to heal our land." I still feel a great debt of gratitude to this wonderful man.

I would challenge the historians here tonight to find any former presidents who, after leaving the White House, have formed a closer and more intimate friendship than Gerald Ford and I. I am grateful for that.

When Rosalynn and I were preparing our move to the White House, we naturally felt some concern and trepidation. We sent two of our staff members from Georgia to find out what we should expect. When they arrived here, the White House staff surrounded them, asking questions about our personal preferences— the times we got up and went to bed, and the kinds of things we liked to eat. When our staff members mentioned our taste for butter beans, collard greens, and cornbread, the head butler turned around to the others and said, "We'll just have to cook a little more of what we have been fixing for our own staff." So that is the kind of food we enjoyed for the four years we lived here.

After the Inaugural Address, which I just mentioned, we sat in a cold pavilion for almost two hours after Rosalynn and I had walked down Pennsylvania Avenue. My mother was with us and our children as we finally started to walk toward the White House. The press corps surrounded our family with television cameras and with microphones, and Jody Powell, who was my press secretary, said, "Don't anybody talk to the press." My mother turned around and said, "Jody, you might tell Jimmy what to do, but as far as I am concerned you can go to hell."

My mother was a democrat with a small "d" and also a large "D," by the way. The first question she got after I made what I thought was a beautiful Inaugural Address was, "Miss Lillian, aren't you proud of your son?" and Mama said, "Which one?"

So that was our introduction to the White House. And it is good for us to think back on the awe-inspiring feeling that I am sure each one of us has had when we moved into this mansion. It's been a part of the life of every president. George Washington conceived it, helped to design it, and supervised its building. Since then all of us have lived here. When it was built, it was the largest house in America. In the last few days I have asked several people, "What do you think is the most famous building in the world?" One said the Taj Mahal. Another one said Buckingham Place. The rest of them said the White House.

Since Rosalynn and I left the White House we have visited 120 nations. In all those countries the White House is recognized as the center of American political life. Quite often people will say, "The White House said" this or that. No one in the world can escape the influence of the decisions made here, by those of us who have served here.

*"In the last few days
I have asked several people,
'What do you think is the
most famous building in
the world?' One said the
Taj Mahal. Another one
said Buckingham Palace.
The rest of them said
the White House."*
—*Jimmy Carter*

I think the White House is special because, as Jerry Ford said so eloquently, it's a combination of things. It's a place to work. Every president since John Adams has had an office here. Abraham Lincoln filled the entire place up with office seekers, and finally limited them to the first floor alone. To go into the rooms and see a small desk that Thomas Jefferson designed himself and carried on the back of his horse when he went from one place to another, or to know that a certain chair or desk was used by a president, to go into the Map Room and see where Franklin Roosevelt and Winston Churchill planned the strategy of the Second World War, where Harry Truman said his prayers or where Richard Nixon said his, is to experience the history of this place.

The White House is a center for awe-inspiring power, even though sometimes the American people exaggerate the power that is concentrated here. President Truman said his biggest surprise was that he gave an order and nothing happened. I think all of us have experienced that, too. Visitors certainly are impressed by the White House. I had a lot of very ambitious people come to see me who had helped me in my campaign from Georgia and other places. They would come into the Oval Office and they would sit there, literally inarticulate. They could not say a word. They would open their mouths, and no sound would come out. I wish more people had been affected that way while I was president! Afterwards my visitors would recover and go to my staff members and tell what brought them here and what they wanted me to grant them.

This place is one of unforgettable personal memories for Rosalynn and me. We moved here when Amy was just nine years old, and we had our sons Jeff and Chip with us with their wives. After we had been here only a month, Chip and his wife presented us with a grandson named James, James Earl Carter IV. He was basically raised

President Jimmy Carter, daughter Amy, and grandson Jason enjoy time in the tree house the president designed himself on the grounds of the White House.

by the White House butlers. When James came back with us this past April, because of the gracious invitation of President Clinton who also invited all of the previous butlers to come back to their duty, we saw many of those who had retired. To see the tears shed when they embraced little James, who is now a senior in college, was indeed heartwarming. We enjoyed our life here.

This afternoon I had a press conference—on my own volition—as a former president who has helped to conduct elections around the world, in countries where democracy was threatened or dictatorship was being replaced by freedom. I have seen troubled elections before, but an uncertain presidential election is an unaccustomed event for Americans. I think that all of us should be confident that our system will prevail, that our nation is so great, so strong, and the tradition is so embedded in the consciousness of all leaders that we will survive this present uncertainty about the outcome of the election.

I had two or three questions from the media. The last question was, "Don't you think it is strange and ironic that, considering what is going on in Florida, you and Bill Clinton will be attending an event tonight with Gerald Ford and George Bush?" I responded, "I think that is a vivid demonstration of what the White House and service in it means to all of us." This was a trenchant question that had to be answered.

All of us have had varying degrees of experiences here. Chuck Robb appeared tonight in the midst of all the former presidents, and we congratulated him on his great service as a senator and consoled him on his recent loss. We could say, "Look around at Gerald Ford, at Jimmy Carter, at George Bush, at Bill Clinton when he was governor, at Lady Bird Johnson whose husband was thought to be victorious in Texas in 1941." All of us lost, so we have learned to experience personal disappointment as well as great honor and achievements as occupants of the White House.

I think the Oval Office in the White House epitomizes for all Americans the stability and the greatness of peace and freedom and democracy and human rights, not only for Americans but also for all people in the world. My dream is that the epitome of the high ideals of humankind, expressed in physical terms in the White House, will continue for another 100 or even 1000 years.

MR. HUGH SIDEY

Thank you very much, President Carter. And now President Bush. I must say tonight, President Bush and Barbara Bush added a chapter once again of great grace under pressure. I am sure their hearts and their minds are somewhat in turmoil and divided on this night, but they have come and they have honored us in this moment. It is really kind of special. You know a couple of years ago when I first suggested to President Bush that we would have a commemoration to mark that day when John Adams moved into the White House, I had no idea he would emulate John Adams to the point of having his son run for president. These things do happen that way. And President Bush, your turn.

PRESIDENT BUSH

Thank you, Hugh. Barbara and I are always honored to return to the White House, and we are grateful, very grateful, to President and Senator Elect Clinton, once again, for their hospitality. We are also pleased to join in saluting the White House Historical Association, and all who organized this evening's festivities.

In 1992, Barbara and I had the great pleasure of hosting the celebration surrounding the 200th anniversary of the laying of the White House cornerstone. Shortly after that occasion, President Reagan came to the White House to receive the Medal of Freedom and, referring to the laying of that cornerstone in 1792, joked, "My back is still killing me."

One of the most gracious men to occupy this house—kinder and gentler, if you will—our thoughts are with Ronald Reagan tonight, and his beloved Nancy. But what a joy to see Lady Bird Johnson and to be with the distinguished men and women who have called this majestic building "home." It might be strange to think of the White House in those terms, but that's exactly what it is to those who have been called to serve here. In this most public of government buildings, amid the ecstasy and agony of history, exists a genuine family home.

Someone once likened living in the White House to living in a fishbowl—but thanks in no small measure to the dedicated professionalism of the White House staff it is possible to have a very happy family life here. And it is possible to protect one's privacy.

For example, when Thomas Jefferson wasn't negotiating the Louisiana Purchase to double the size of our young nation westward and grappling with European belligerence in the sea-lanes of the Atlantic to the east, he played the fiddle, and he taught his pet mockingbird to peck food from his lips, and Jefferson even taught the bird to hop up the staircase after him. What a sight that must have been!

Here, too, Harry Truman set in motion the events that would secure the Allied victory in the twilight of World War II and set in place the foundation of a policy of containment in the early dawn of the cold war—even as he dealt with the nocturnal mischief by the infamous White House ghosts. And for the record: in the best of the American spirit, even the haunting of the White House was bipartisan. John Quincy Adams and Abraham Lincoln from the Federalist/Republican tradition, and Andrew Jackson and Polk, James Polk, for the Democrats—all reportedly gave Harry hell.

As for President Adams, when he first opened the doors here to do the country's business, not only were the conditions he discovered primitive at best, but there was no official White House staff to assist him. It would be a cold and lonely winter for the mansion's first

"Age and the elements occasionally wear her down, but this house is forever renewed by the ageless fidelity of its Founders and the boundless promise of its future heirs."
—*George Bush*

resident. Complicating an already trying circumstance for Adams, a Federalist, was the fact that, by a long since abolished provision in the election of 1796, he was the only president forced to serve with a vice president from an opposition political party—Thomas Jefferson, the Democratic-Republican. Perhaps the only other man to endure such an "uncomfortable" arrangement here was President Truman, who spent most of his presidency living with his mother-in-law!

And speaking of interesting election outcomes, as this week's presidential contest wound down, much was made in the media of this potential historical parallel between the Adams and the Bush families—and for once I am compelled to say the press is far more prescient than previously thought possible. The election of 2000, pitting the son of a president against a candidate from Tennessee, is destined to join the election of 1824, with the same personal dynamic, as one of the closest in our nation's history. Whatever happens this year, my pride and Barbara's pride knows no bounds. Moreover, our democracy will endure, as President Carter said, and the new president will become part of the continuum of service that sets our nation, and this building, apart.

Like the stonecutters who chiseled their banker-marks into the stones that form this house, the new president will leave his mark here. Together with the new first lady, they will write the next chapter in the history of the White House, proving that the names and faces may change, but this house, like our beloved republic, endures.

Many years ago Henry Longfellow foretold our country's proud destiny in confident terms with his epic "Ship of State," which in my view is an apt description for the White House. More often than not, it necessarily falls to this vessel of statecraft to set the pace and lead the way, and push on to the frontiers of progress and prosperity and peace.

Surrounded by family photos in the Oval Office, President George Bush makes a point to granddaughter Marshall Bush.

For 200 years and eight days this old house has been buffeted by the winds of change and battered by the troubled waters of war. We have been favored by calm seas, too, but history tells us that democracy thrives when the gusts and gales of challenge and adversity fill its sails and compel it into action. And through it all—through trial and tribulation, as well as triumph—the White House has served as our nation's anchor to windward, a vision of constancy, a fortress of freedom, the repository of a billion American dreams. Age and the elements occasionally wear her down, but this house is forever renewed by the ageless fidelity of its Founders and the boundless promise of its future heirs.

In the immortal words of Longfellow, "Sail on, O Ship of State. Sail on, O Union, strong and great!"

MR. HUGH SIDEY

Now it's to our host, President Clinton. He faces one more formidable task that perhaps is not on the agenda for a president winding down his time in that's he is going to have to face the world without Air Force One. And I have heard the testimony of many who have left, and it's no small hardship. I think he will make it.

You know, over these years I have talked to the president—not that often, but every time we have somehow talked about history, of walking down the corridors among the portraits of the great people who have preceded him and learning the stories of their successes and their trials. And I remember one evening he took a group of us around his study desk, which was Ulysses S. Grant's cabinet table, and explained that each of the cabinet officers sat around there, and they had one drawer for their papers— one little drawer in a nation that was suddenly becoming a huge industrial power. Well, we have come a long way from there. And I remember President Clinton saying, "I've changed my mind about some of these people. Once you are here, once you are in this, the world seems different." So, President Clinton, tell us a little bit about it. Thank you.

PRESIDENT CLINTON

I want to thank Lady Bird Johnson and President and Mrs. Ford, President and Mrs. Carter, and President and Mrs. Bush for being here. I thought that joke about Harry Truman living with his mother-in-law was particularly apt. My mother-in-law is upstairs at this very moment, and she has agreed to let me live with her for the next two years when I am in Arkansas trying to establish my library.

I, like previous speakers, would like to acknowledge President and Mrs. Reagan and say that we miss them and wish them well. I would also like to acknowledge a person who's been a particular friend of Hillary's and mine these last eight years who suffered two losses in her family recently and could not be here tonight, but about whom we care very much, Margaret Truman Daniel, and we are thinking of her and wishing her well. I would like to thank Senator and Mrs. Robb for being here, and for their service to America. And I would like to thank you, General Eisenhower, thank you for coming. We are honored to have you here. And Ethel Kennedy, thank you for coming. And other members of presidents' families.

One of the most interesting things to me about living here these last eight years is watching the threads of American history weave their ways through the families of presidents. The other day we held a ceremony here commemorating the 200th anniversary of the opening of the White House. An actor played John Adams, and he came up with a footman, his horses, and an old 18th-century carriage, and he got out. And then we had a little reception for all of the Adams family members in the direct line of John and John Quincy Adams who were here. It turned out that one of them had two sons in the United States Navy today, one of whom serves on a destroyer that is a twin to the USS *Cole*. He was there when Hillary and I spoke with the families at the memorial service a few days ago. It made me once again very grateful to be an American as well as to have the opportunity to live here.

I thank the members of the White House Historical Association and especially Bob Breeden and Hugh Sidey. Hugh, I hope you won't mind. You have had some fun at our expense. I was thinking there—for at least two of us up here at the table—you have said more nice things about us tonight than you have throughout our public life! We are immensely grateful. I was also thinking that between us, we have served so long that we have been here about half as long as Helen Thomas. We are delighted to see you. I want to thank the members of the Marine Band. You know I was a band boy in high school, which, if you were from Arkansas and over 6 feet tall, was a bad thing to be. But I loved music from the time I was a child, and I think it would be fair to say that I doubt that any president has enjoyed the Marine Band as much as I have. I have loved every encounter I have had with them, and they are absolutely magnificent.

I know that all of you have noticed that every president who has spoken here tonight has thanked Gary Walters and the White House residence staff. They were not going through the motions. They were not saying that because that was something they had to say. Until you have lived here and you realize how totally bizarre your life can get from time to time, it's impossible to express how grateful you are to people who make it normal and who, no matter what, who are always there for you at all hours of the day and night, when you are up in the polls and down in the polls, when you are celebrating your greatest triumph or the wheel runs off—and they still try to make it a home. Then when you have to get out and make it a public place simultaneously, they do that as well. So to Gary and from you to all the people who are down in the basement tonight keeping the lights on, making sure that the temperature works, all of the people you never see, to all of these wonderful people who served our dinner tonight, we thank you from the bottom of our hearts. Thank you.

History tells us that even as the city's planners debated the final design of this house, the masons laid its stone foundations 4 feet thick. Like our nation's Founders, these men were building a monument to freedom that they wanted to last. Now, over the course of

Chelsea Clinton plays with her cat Socks in the Oval Office while waiting for her father to join her for a Christmas shopping trip.

two centuries, as all of you know and we have seen some references tonight, this old house has withstood war and fire and bulldozers, just as its inhabitants have faced a stern test or two.

In this remarkable audience there are former residents, historians, and others who have very little to learn about the White House. But I thought I would use, if I might, the story of the East Room (where we are now tonight) as just a metaphor. You have already heard that the East Room began its existence as Abigail Adams's laundry room. But soon after that, carpenters partitioned two boxlike rooms of wood framing and fabric for explorer Meriwether Lewis's use in the south end of the East Room. One room served as his office, and the other was his bedchamber. Lewis served as President Thomas Jefferson's secretary and, more important, his pupil for his role in a great western exploration that would be known as the Lewis and Clark expedition.

Whether you agree with all of Thomas Jefferson's policies or not, it's interesting that just in buying Louisiana and launching the Lewis and Clark expedition he helped to make us the great continental nation that we are today. A few years after that, President Lincoln introduced Ulysses Grant to well wishers at an East Room reception. You may remember that a lot of people in Washington didn't like General Grant. He was 5 feet 4 inches, unimposing; he forgot to shave on some days when he was more interested in battle. And he was said to enjoy a drink from time to time. And when some of the people here in Washington were criticizing this rube from the hinterland because of his drinking habits, President Lincoln wryly suggested that he wished the person would find out what General Grant drank and give it to the other generals. It might end the war more quickly.

In fact, that is one of the many things that are untrue. There is not a single document providing evidence that General Grant was ever drunk on the job. I thought I would use this historic moment to clean this slate a little bit. But, anyway, Grant was a little guy, and they were mobbing him here in this room. So he did something that I am not sure I would have the courage to do. He jumped up on the sofa and stood there so he would not be completely overrun by the crowd. It was here more tragically that, just a couple of years later, Abraham Lincoln lay in state.

And here, quite fittingly, a century later President Lyndon Johnson signed the Civil Rights Act, one of the most important American acts of the last 50 years. Just 25 years ago Gerald Ford took the oath of office and was sworn in as president here. We have had so many happy nights here, but I think I will just mention one because the person who made it so happy is here in this room.

Not so very long ago we celebrated the 50th anniversary of the North Atlantic Treaty Organization, the embodiment of our commitment in the cold war to stand against communism. And on that occasion we had this marvelous dinner with an arched head table with all the heads of state, the largest number of heads of state to ever visit Washington at one time. They were entertained here by Jessye Norman, standing and singing alone. We welcome you here again tonight. Thank you very much.

This place is a thrill to live in. You heard President Carter say that he told them he wanted to eat the things that the staff were eating. When I came here, we asked them to redo the kitchen so that we could have dinner in the kitchen at night. Just about every night for eight years Hillary and Chelsea and I have had dinner in the little kitchen upstairs—which is interesting how low standards have sunk! Until Jackie and John Kennedy moved here, first families came downstairs to dine, in a formal dining room, every night for 160 years. Who knows, maybe the next crowd will be eating on the roof!

We have enjoyed being in the Solarium where President Reagan convalesced after he was shot. We have enjoyed the company of family and friends there. And I've spent a lot of my evenings alone working in the Treaty Room, as you just heard from Hugh Sidey, on the great walnut table that President Grant used for a cabinet table. It was in that same room, which was Abraham Lincoln's waiting room, on that table, that the protocol to the treaty ending the Spanish-American War

was signed in 1898. Thereafter it became known as the Treaty Table, and many historic treaties signed in the United States in 102 years have been signed on that table—President Carter's Camp David Accords, the treaty signed by Yitzhak Rabin and King Hussein of Jordan ending the war between their two nations. It always reminds me that I am a temporary resident.

Hillary and Chelsea and I will be forever grateful to the American people for letting us make the White House our home for what was, as I find amazing now, 40 percent of my daughter's young life. The day we moved in, Hillary devoted herself to preserving the White House, to the restoration of public rooms, to the selection of the bicentennial china we used tonight, to installing sculpture in the Jacqueline Kennedy Garden. I thank her for the work she has done to make this a more vibrant living museum than ever. I thank Mrs. Carter and Mrs. Bush for the work they did, which Hillary was able to help complete, to adequately endow the White House Endowment Fund so that this house and its collections will be better preserved for all future visitors and so that all people who come here will better understand our nation's past. Now soon we, too, will be part of that past.

When I leave here, as we all must, I will depart with a great, deep sense of gratitude, and I am being helped along the way by all my friends who are determined to keep me humble and grounded. The other day I went to a meeting of the bishops of the Church of God and Christ, and I thought I was being quite clever. I got up in front of these 400 bishops and I said I wanted to come here today because I wanted to be among some leaders who aren't term-limited. And the head bishop got up and said, "O Mr. President, we are all term-limited."

And so I say tonight, the White House has never belonged to any one of us. It will always belong to all of us. We do not yet know who the next occupant will be. But we can honor the service, the lives, and the families of the candidates who contested this election. We know how proud President and Mrs. Bush must be of their son, and rightly so. And we Americans should take great pride in the fact that this contest was fought to a close conclusion. It is not a symbol of the division of our nation, but the vitality of our debate. And it will be resolved in a way consonant with the vitality of our enduring Constitution and laws.

I think tonight of the words of an Englishman, Charles Dickens, who visited here in 1842. Listen to what he said right after he attended one of the functions that they then called "levees." Where I come from, that holds in the Mississippi River. But for years in the 19th century, the receptions that presidents regularly held were called levees. Dickens walked through the White House listening to the Marine Band play, marveling at the crowd assembled. Here is how he described the event in his *American Notes:* "Every man even among the miscellaneous crowd in the hall who were admitted without any orders or tickets to look on appeared to feel that he was part of the institution."

Well, that is still the way it ought to be. Every one of you, from the wealthiest to those who could not be called wealthy, of whatever race or region, whatever your background, whether you are dining here or are working here, you are a part of the institution. You are the center of the nation. The most important title in this house has ever been and will always be "citizen." That is, after all, why we are still around after 200 years. Thank you, and God bless you.

PRESIDENT REAGAN

President Ronald Reagan, suffering from Alzheimer's disease, was

the only living president unable to attend the 200th anniversary dinner.

But before he was stricken with the disease he talked about his days in

the White House in an interview with Hugh Sidey. Here is an excerpt

from that interview.

I was amazed by how comfortable it was to live in the White House.

Over the years there has been a lot of rebuilding, a lot of changing.

But it works. I was once reading a history of the house… and of all the

presidents who had come in and wanted to change the furniture

and sell the furniture and have new things. And one Sunday morning

I was sitting upstairs alone and I finished the book…. I put the book

down and I started walking through every room of the White House

as if I were seeing it for the first time. But as I went I was remembering

where this room was changed and then changed back again…. it was

a new view of the White House and I was just fascinated.

This rare formal portrait of all the living presidents and first ladies, with the exception of the Reagans, was taken to commemorate the 200th anniversary dinner at the White House.

First ladies sitting left to right: Barbara Bush, Lady Bird Johnson, Hillary Rodham Clinton, Betty Ford, and Rosalynn Carter.

Presidents standing left to right: George Bush, William J. Clinton, Gerald R. Ford, and Jimmy Carter.

Music

Following the dinner, President and Mrs. Clinton invited guests to the Entrance Hall to enjoy music from the United States Marine Band. The Marine Band, which has performed at the White House since 1801, presented the inaugural performance of "The President's House: A Bicentennial Tribute," composed by John Tatgenhorst.

The United States Marine Band is America's oldest professional musical organization. Its primary mission is unique—to provide music for the president of the United States. Whether performing for South Lawn arrival ceremonies, state dinners, or receptions, Marine Band musicians appear at the White House nearly 200 times each year.

Music has been a part of life in the White House from the earliest days of our nation, making its White House debut at President and Mrs. John Adams's New Year's Day reception in 1801. Present at many of the most memorable and cherished moments in our nation's history, the band played for the dedication of the National Cemetery at Gettysburg when President Lincoln gave his immortal address. It has provided music for every inauguration since the time of Thomas Jefferson, the president who gave it the title, "the President's Own."

The Marine Band was
the first musical ensemble to
perform at the White House.
The sheet music for its
"Bicentennial Tribute"
is pictured at left in the
Red Room.

"The excellence of their performance makes them a welcome and important part of state functions. The Marine Band deserves every recognition and accolade they receive."
—President Gerald R. Ford

"The only problem is that Mr. Hamlisch wants to take my Marine Band back with him. He can't have them!"
—President Jimmy Carter, remarks following a South Lawn performance of Rodgers and Hammerstein's *Carousel*

"For 185 years the White House has been filled with our most American of sounds, the music of the United States Marine Band. Congratulations to you, I am proud to call you 'the President's Own.'"
—President Ronald Reagan

"Your music inspired me and often made me shed a tear of gratitude for those who serve the nation in uniform."
—President George Bush

"When I leave this job, I'll miss a lot of things about Washington and the White House and a few things I won't. But I'll really miss the Marine Band."
—President William J. Clinton

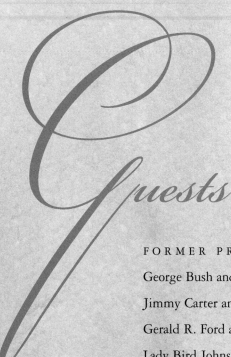

Guests

FORMER PRESIDENTS AND FIRST LADIES

George Bush and Barbara Bush

Jimmy Carter and Rosalynn Carter

Gerald R. Ford and Betty Ford

Lady Bird Johnson

DINNER GUESTS

Benjamin Adams, President, Adams Memorial Society, and Jennifer Adams

Madeleine K. Albright, Secretary of State, and Evelyn Lieberman

William Allman, Assistant Curator, The White House, and Barbara McMillan

Leonore Annenberg, Committee for the Preservation of the White House

Carl Sferrazza Anthony, historian, and Richard Sullivan

Samuel Berger, National Security Adviser, and Susan Berger

Michael Beschloss, White House Historical Association,
        and Afsaneh Mashayekhi Beschloss

James H. Billington, Librarian of Congress, and Marjorie Billington

Taylor Branch, author, and Jed Dietz

Robert L. Breeden, Chairman, White House Historical Association,
        and Cynthia B. Scudder

J. Carter Brown, Chairman, U.S. Commission of Fine Arts

Iris Cantor, philanthropist, and John Desiderio

John W. Carlin, Archivist of the United States, and Lynn Carlin

Nash Castro, White House Historical Association, and Bette W. Castro

Charles M. Cawley, Chairman and CEO, MBNA New England, and Julie Cawley

Jeannine Smith Clark, White House Historical Association, and Dr. Charles H. Clark

William Cohen, Secretary of Defense, and Janet Langhart Cohen

Donald J. Crump, White House Historical Association

Maria J. Downs, White House Historical Association, and John E. Downs

Henry A. Dudley Jr., White House Historical Association, and Ann Dudley

John Eisenhower, author, and Joanne Eisenhower

George M. Elsey, White House Historical Association

Anthony Essaye, attorney, and Anne Essaye

Mrs. Johnson blows a kiss to the crowd as President Bush joins in the applause.

John Fahey Jr., White House Historical Association, and Heidi Fahey

Jonathan Fairbanks, Committee for the Preservation of the White House,
and Louisa Fairbanks

Pam Fleischaker, U.S. Holocaust Memorial Council, and David Fleischaker

Nancy M. Folger, White House Historical Association, and Sidney Werkman

Carson M. Glass, White House Historical Association, and Wilma Jo Bush

Cathy Gorn, White House Historical Association, and Richard T. Prasse

Betsy Gotbaum, New-York Historical Society, and Victor Gotbaum

Katharine Graham, Chairman of the Executive Committee, Washington Post Company

David I. Granger, White House Historical Association, and Mary R. Granger

Charles Guggenheim, White House Historical Association, and Marion Guggenheim

Henry Haller, former White House Executive Chef, and Carole Haller

John Hardman, Carter Center

Helen Hartzog and Edward A. Hartzog

Alexis Herman, Secretary of Labor, and Charles Franklin

Kaki Hockersmith, Committee for the Preservation of the White House, and Max Mehlburger

Neil W. Horstman, White House Historical Association, and Anne H. Horstman

Janice M. Johnson, Committee for the Preservation of the White House, and Roger W. Johnson

Vernon Jordan, attorney, and Ann Jordan

Ethel Kennedy and Christopher Kennedy

Elise K. Kirk, White House Historical Association, and Graham Down

William Kloss, Committee for the Preservation of the White House, and Charles Timbrell

Norman Lear, Act III Communications, and Maggie Lear

Gerald M. Levin, Time Warner Inc.

Maya Lin, architect, and Daniel Wolf

Ellen M. Lovell, Director, White House Millennium Council, and Christopher Lovell

Terry McAuliffe, American Heritage Homes, and Dorothy McAuliffe

James I. McDaniel, White House Liaison, National Park Service, and Michele McDaniel

*President Clinton
with Edward A. Hartzog
and Helen Hartzog*

Nancy M. Folger and Sidney Werkman

Chelsea Clinton

Leon B. Polsky, Anne Sidey, and Gary Walters

Elizabeth Taylor and William Rollnick

J. Carter Brown

Theodora Taylor, Billy Taylor, and Elise K. Kirk

Floretta Dukes McKenzie, White House Historical Association, and Kedrick N. Kilpatrick

Bernard R. Meyer, White House Historical Association

Norman Mineta, Secretary of Commerce, and Deni Mineta

Richard Moe, Committee for the Preservation of the White House, and Julia Moe

Set Charles Momjian, former U.S. Representative to the United Nations, and Joan Momjian

Betty Monkman, Curator, The White House

Roger Mudd, History Channel, and E. J. Mudd

Jessye Norman, opera singer, and David Kleinberg

Richard Nylander, Committee for the Preservation of the White House, and Jane Nylander

Marianne Peak, Adams National Historic Site, and Alexandra Peak

John Podesta, Chief of Staff to the President, and Michele Ballantyne

Philippa Polskin, Ruder Finn Arts, and Howard Polskin

Cynthia Hazen Polsky and Leon B. Polsky

Roger B. Porter, White House Historical Association, and Ann Porter

Jessye Norman and Vernon Jordan

Earl A. Powell III, Director, National Gallery of Art, and Courtney Powell

Rita J. Pynoos, Smithsonian Institution, and Morris S. Pynoos

Steven Ricchetti, Assistant to the President and Deputy Chief of Staff, and Amy Blanchard Ricchetti

John L. Richardson, Committee for the Preservation of the White House, and Margaret Milner Richardson

Richard Riley, Secretary of Education, and Tunky Riley

Charles Robb, Senator, and Lynda Johnson Robb

William Rollnick, Mattel Inc., and Nancy Ellison

Ramon Eduardo Ruiz, University of California at San Diego, and Natalia Ruiz

Shirley Sagawa, Deputy Assistant to the President, and Gregory Baer

President and Mrs. Carter

John Carlin and Floretta Dukes McKenzie

Elaine W. Silverstein

Roger W. Sant, AES Corp., and Vicki Sant

J. Thomas Savage Jr., Committee for the Preservation of the White House,
    and Margaret Pritchard

Lie Schiffer, attorney, and Rosalie S. Gould

Arthur Schlesinger Jr., historian, and Alexandra Emmet Schlesinger

William Seale, historian, and Lucinda Seale

Donna Shalala, Secretary of Health and Human Services

Walter Shorenstein, philanthropist, and Clotilde Alvarez

Hugh S. Sidey, President, White House Historical Association, and Anne Sidey

Leonard L. Silverstein, White House Historical Association, and Elaine W. Silverstein

Stephen A. Simon and Bonnie Ward Simon

Linda Hohenfeld Slatkin, soprano, National Symphony Orchestra, and Michael T. Gafford

Donna Hayashi Smith, Office of the Curator, The White House, and Michael Smith

Alfred R. Stern, White House Historical Association, and Barbara Biben

Ann Stock, Kennedy Center, and Tracy LaBrecque Davis

Lawrence Summers, Secretary of the Treasury, and Sheryl Sandberg

Billy Taylor, pianist, and Theodora Taylor

Elizabeth Taylor, actress, and Cary Schwartz

Helen Thomas, columnist, and Charles J. Lewis

Susan P. Thomases, White House Historical Association, and William Bettridge

Melanne Verveer, Assistant to the President, and Philip Louis Verveer

Gary Walters, Chief Usher, The White House

Diane Simmons Williams, Greater Washington Urban League, and Asantwa Foster

Maggie Williams, Fenton Communications, and William Barrett

John Wilmerding, Committee for the Preservation of the White House, and Lila W. Kirkland

Mary Ellen Withrow, Treasurer of the United States

Jamie Wyeth, artist, and Phyllis Wyeth

COMMENT BY WALTER SCHEIB III, CHEF OF THE WHITE HOUSE

This was a tremendous opportunity to do research on the food—flavor combinations, the cooking techniques, and the ingredients—that were available 200 years ago in the Washington area. Even though good restaurants today always talk about local and seasonal, 200 years ago if it wasn't local and seasonal you didn't have it. There wasn't delivery across the country. A lot of the items you see on the menu are really mid-Atlantic. In many cases, the dinner reflects a contemporary menu for the time of the year in that the same principles of seasonality and locality were in play both in 1800 and today.

The first course was a duck consommé, and at this time of the year there are a lot of waterfowl in transit. According to the research, primarily of Jeffersonian dining style, game was one of his specialties at this time of year. So we made a nice consommé of duck, and we have winter or root vegetables—parsnips, turnips, carrots—that have been roasted and added to the consommé with Madeira wine, which was mentioned several times in Jefferson's writings.

The fish course was a seared striped bass. Anyone who knows the Washington area knows that the striped bass is the fish of the Chesapeake Bay and migrates well up the Potomac River. Accompanying this was a fricassee of corn and crab—blue crab specifically. The sauce was a reduction of vermouth and oysters cooked down and finished with a chive purée. The oysters were very typical of this area.

The entrée was peppered grilled lamb with a light smoke on it. Smoking and

Executive Chef Walter Scheib in the White House kitchen with his assistants. Left to right: Rachel Walker, John Moeller, Walter Scheib, Chris Comerford, and Adam Collick.

curing were two of the techniques that were used 200 years ago, when preservation was necessary and refrigeration wasn't what it is today. We haven't cured the lamb to the point of preservation, but there is a light smoke in it as a tip of the hat to that tradition. We went out and found some heirloom apples that were first planted in the early 1800s in York, Pennsylvania. They are small and not cosmetically attractive, but they have a tremendous big apple flavor and are tart. When you cook them down, they have a wonderful flavor. They were used as a thickening agent in the sauce, so there was no flour or cream to thicken the sauce. It was actually done with an apple purée.

For the cheese course with the salad, we found an artisan who was making cheeses as they did 200 years ago. They were all made from unpasteurized cow's milk and wild-ripened, which means they were ripened by the existing yeasts and spores in the air as opposed to many cultured cheeses that are actually inoculated to get their cure. We took a fig marmalade, which was one of the major ways these fruits were preserved, and cooked it down with sugar and seasonings to a jam consistency and layered that with this cheese. Poached pear was put over the top. It was fruity and tangy together. We have a variety of winter greens—endives, spinaches—that will go well with this. The dressing is based on the fig marmalade with the addition of balsamic vinegar and a little lemon and olive oil.

It was great fun putting this menu together. For once we were able to look backward and discover some interesting recipe ideas, instead of trying to look ahead and find the next new challenge. —*Walter Scheib III, November 9, 2000*

DINNER

In celebration of
The 200th Anniversary
of The White House

Truffle and Duck Consommé
Roasted Vegetables and Madeira

Seared Striped Bass
Corn and Crab Fricassee
Chive and Oyster Sauce

Grapefruit and Gin Sherbet

Smoked Loin of Lamb
Heirloom Apples, Butternut Squash and Salsify

Terrine of Pears, Figs and Wild Ripened Cheese
Winter Greens
Fig Dressing

Abigail Adams' Floating Island
Raisin Biscuits
Lemon Bars

Kistler Chardonnay "Cuvee Cathleen" 1996
Landmark Pinot Noir "Kastania Vineyard" 1997
Bonny Doon "Vin Glaciere Muscat" 1999

The White House
Thursday, November 9, 2000

The following recipes are selections from the
menu on page 101. They are not intended as
instructions for preparing complete courses.

SELECTED RECIPES

RAVIOLI FILLING AND PRODUCTION TO ACCOMPANY THE DUCK CONSOMME

4 oz. duck confit
(recipe follows)
pasta dough
(recipe follows)

4 oz. total fine diced parsnip, turnip,
carrot, celery root

2–3 oz. duck demiglace (duck stock
reduced by $3/4$ until syrupy in
consistency) with Madiera added
to taste

$1/2$ oz. fine-diced truffles

1 tablespoon white truffle oil

1 tablespoon roasted garlic purée

1 oz. fine-diced shallots

1) Finely dice or shred the duck leg confit
removing skin and tendons. Saute
in pan quickly to slightly carmelize.
Set aside to cool.

2) In hot pan, sauté diced root vegetables
until slightly carmelized, then add
shallots. Cook until they are soft.
Season with salt and pepper. Remove
this mixture from pan and cool.

3) To this mixture add very briefly
sautéed truffle dice, roasted garlic
purée, truffle oil.

4) Combine cool vegetable mix. Cool
duck meat in bowl. Add slightly
warmed demiglace, enough to coat
and bind. Adjust seasonings.

5) Roll out pasta dough to the thickness
desired (the thinner the better).

6) Brush pasta sheet lightly with
beaten egg wash.

7) Evenly space (about 2 inches apart)
dime-size dabs of duck filling onto
the pasta sheet, covering only half of
the dough. Then fold uncovered half
over filling dabs. With a one-inch
circle cutter, form upper dough down
over filling to seal with lower dough.
Press well to ensure tight seal,
then cut.

8) Hold ravioli cool and covered
until service.

9) Cook ravioli in a gently boiling
salted water (or preferably
consommé) until they are just cooked.
Add to consommé at service.

This silver tea or coffee urn
(c. 1785–88) was owned by
John and Abigail Adams and is
now displayed in the Green Room
of the White House.

DUCK CONFIT

4 tablespoons coarse kosher salt

1 tablespoon pepper mignonette

1 tablespoon chopped garlic

1 tablespoon chopped Italian parsley

1 bay leaf, crumbled

2 cups rendered duck fat

2–3 lbs. duck legs

1) Combine the salt, pepper, garlic,
   parsley, and bay leaf in a bowl.
   Rub the duck legs with the mixture,
   lay on a rack to cure in the
   refrigerator at least 24 hours.

2) Bring the duck fat to a slow simmer.

3) Rinse the duck legs and carefully
   arrange into the pot with fat. Confit
   for about 3 hours, until the meat is
   fork tender. Cool the duck and store
   refrigerated up to two weeks.

   Yield: 4 servings

PASTA DOUGH

Soup tureen and stand and preserves stand from the dinner service made in France in 1782 that belonged to John and Abigail Adams.

3 cups semolina flour

    (for soft, more pliable dough,

    reduce semolina and add all-

    purpose flour in an equal amount)

1 teaspoon salt

4 large eggs

4 tablespoons water

4 tablespoons olive oil

1) Sift salt and flour together.

2) Beat together eggs, water, and oil.

3) Form well in flour on table. Pour liquid into well, stir liquid to incorporate flour bit by bit. (Or combine all ingredients in mixing machine.)

4) When fairly stiff and elastic dough forms, knead well for 10 minutes.

5) Set dough aside, covered, and let rest at least 30 minutes.

CHIVE AND OYSTER SAUCE TO ACCOMPANY SEARED STRIPED BASS

This plate is from the state service commissioned by Ronald and Nancy Reagan in 1981.

12 oz. leek whites

2 oz. shallots

$^1/_2$ oz. garlic

2 oz. celery

2–3 oz. Dry Vermouth

3–4 oz. fish fumet—

   made from sole bones

2–4 (per person) freshly shucked

   oysters with liquor reserved

1–2 oz. reduced heavy cream

1 oz. whole butter

$^1/_2$–1 oz. chive purée—chives blended

   and puréed in blender, then strained

1) Finely cut leeks, shallots, garlic, celery. Sweat lightly until just tender (no color).

2) Deglaze with Vermouth and reduce.

3) Add oysters and liquor and fish fumet.

4) Simmer lightly to cook all flavor from oysters (about 10–12 minutes).

5) Purée above items and pass through fine chinoise.

6) Reduce liquid slightly. Add reduced cream to achieve sauce consistency. Finish by whipping in whole butter, and adjust seasoning.

7) At service, quickly whisk into sauce enough chive purée to get light pastel color.

BRAISED HEIRLOOM APPLES AND BUTTERNUT SQUASH

TO ACCOMPANY SMOKED LOIN OF LAMB

The floral design on this dessert plate from the service commissioned by Lyndon and Lady Bird Johnson reflects the first lady's interest in nature.

3–4 oz. lamb demiglace infused with
    ginger, cinnamon, garlic, and red wine

6 oz. heirloom cooking-style apples,
    peeled and diced (or other cooking-
    style apple)

4 oz. peeled, diced butternut squash

2 oz. diced shallots

2 oz. Reisling wine

1) Saute shallots in hot pan.

2) Add butternut squash. Cook quickly to
slightly color (don't overcook or overstir).

3) Add diced apples and toss quickly.

4) Deglaze with Reisling wine and reduce.

5) Add lamb sauce to just moisten.

6) Cover, reduce heat to low. Cook until
    squash and apples are just tender.
    Adjust seasonings.

7) Serve with some of the unabsorbed
    sauce as base to lamb or game entrée.

POACHED MISSION FIGS TO ACCOMPANY TERRINE OF PEARS AND FIGS

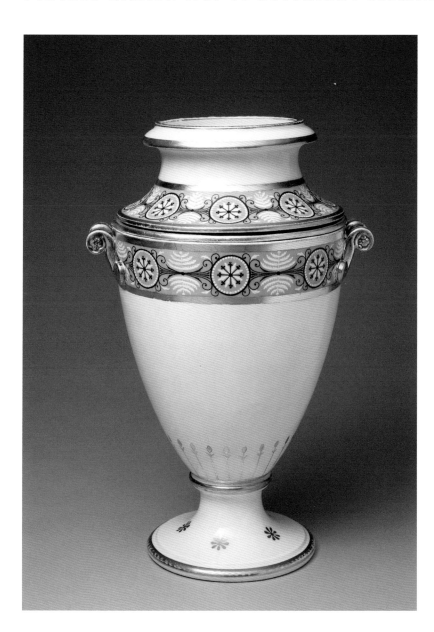

1 pint black mission figs

1 cup grape juice

1 cup Port wine

1 cup Cabernet

1 lemon, zest and juice

$^1/_2$ cup sugar

bay leaf

cinnamon sticks

5 cloves

1) Steep all the ingredients, except

   the figs, for at least an hour.

   Bring to a simmer.

2) Poach the figs for about 5 minutes.

   Cool and refrigerate in the liquid

   until ready to use.

Yield: 1 pint

This dessert cooler (c. 1806)
belongs to a service used by
James and Dolley Madison.

Table Service

*The pattern for gilded silver
forks was selected by First
Lady Frances Cleveland in
1894. Her forks and others
of the same pattern are still
used for state occasions.*

The tables in the East Room were set with the service plates from the Clinton state service. This 200th anniversary service incorporates architectural motifs inspired by details in the State Dining Room, East Room, and Diplomatic Reception Room. (The head table used this service during each course.) At the other tables the Franklin D. Roosevelt state service was used for the first course, the Harry S. Truman state service for the second course, the Lyndon B. Johnson state service for the third course, and the Ronald W. Reagan state service for the fourth course and for dessert.

Gilded silver flatware and glassware of the pattern selected by Jacqueline Kennedy were set on gold damask tablecloths. The floral centerpieces were reminiscent of arrangements one might have found in the White House 200 years ago. Tall gold taper candles and votive candles completed the centerpieces.

COMMENT BY BY NANCY CLARKE, WHITE HOUSE FLORIST

The centerpieces of the early 19th century usually were made of fruits,
vegetables, and flowers from the garden. The source of light at the table was,
of course, candlelight. When Abigail Adams returned from London in 1788,
she brought back a creamy white rose named York. This rose is still growing at
the Adams National Historic Site in Quincy, Massachusetts. I incorporated a white
(actually cream) garden rose from California as a representation of this rose in the
anniversary dinner table centerpieces. The centerpieces were a combination of a
more contemporary style of flower arrangement mixed with the historical use of
fruits and garden greenery. We used a combination of green grapes, limes, and
flowers, including cream roses, soft yellow roses, gardenias, hydrangea, and
Denrobium orchids.

*The garden
rose was used
in the centerpiece
at each table.*

Wine Selection

First Course
Kistler Chardonnay
Cuvée Cathleen, 1996

Main Course
Kastania Pinot Noir
Landmark Vineyard, 1997

Located on the Sonoma Coast region of California, the winery produces a Chardonnay rich in fruit with a light cardamom flavor characterized by a firm, tight structure that results from the cold climate of the region.

Landmark's Pinot Noir yields a wine of lush fruit redolent of black cherry and sage hints. Full bodied and long in finish, it is reminiscent of the Burgundies noted in the diaries kept by President Jefferson and served in his White House.

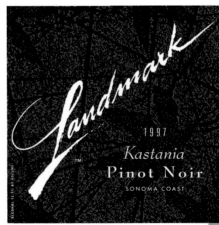

Dessert Course

Vin de Glacière Muscat, 1999

Bonny Doon

This unique wine is reminiscent of the
Sauterne wines served with multiple desserts
in the early White House. The grapes are
grown in a warmer area of California, left to
hang longer than usual for a Muscat wine,
increasing the sugar content, and then,
when picked, quickly frozen in freezers.
The frozen grapes are pressed, producing a
concentrated syrup that is fermented and
filtered to create a wine of copious fruit
hinting of pineapple, peach, pear, and litchi.

The Red Room, 2000.
The cylinder desk and
bookcase, at left, and the
pair of vases on the mantel
are anniversary gifts to the
White House from the
White House Historical
Association.

Gifts

When John and Abigail Adams occupied the White House in 1800, they made do with worn furniture from the Washington administration that had been transported from Philadelphia to the nation's new capital. The Adamses had plans for further acquisitions for the commodious house but their stay was cut short by the election of Thomas Jefferson. Between 1789 and 1961, congressional appropriations and private gifts provided funding for furnishings for the President's House. Congress also authorized the president to auction and sell obsolete or outdated household goods and to use the proceeds to furnish the White House as he saw fit. No abiding system directed the purchase or selection of furniture and artwork, and this arrangement was bound to result in transient decors expressing the personal tastes of the first families.

A significant change occurred in 1961 when Congress enacted legislation declaring that the furnishings of the White House were the inalienable property of the White House and the collections were made permanent. The White House would become a museum of American history and art. Yet adequate federal funding did not follow. In that same year the White House Historical Association was founded. One of the association's primary missions is to support the acquisition of appropriate furnishings and artworks for the public rooms. The association is honored to be able to contribute to the White House collections of fine and decorative arts so that these historically significant and aesthetically beautiful works may be shared with visitors from around the globe. A selection of major gifts to the White House from the White House Historical Association over the course of four decades appears on pages 144–47.

CLINTON STATE SERVICE

In commemoration of the 200th anniversary of the White House, the White House Historical Association donated a new state service to the White House. At the suggestion of Hillary Rodham Clinton, White House architectural motifs were the inspiration for the designs on the individual pieces, and the image of the White House was placed on the service plates and dinner and dessert plates—the first time that the White House has been used on a state service. Other services have used the Presidential Seal, the Great Seal of the United States, or elements of the Great Seal, such as the American eagle or shield. There are 300 place settings in the service; five display sets were ordered, one each for the White House collection, the Smithsonian Institution, President and Mrs. Clinton, the Clinton Library, and Lenox. Each place setting has a service plate, dinner plate, luncheon/fish plate, salad plate, dessert plate, soup plate, cream soup cup and saucer, bouillon cup and saucer, and coffee cup and saucer. All are marked on the reverse: The White House/200th anniversary/1800–2000.

The service plates with the north view of the White House in gold at the center, have a wide, acid-etched, gilt border with a raised design of the wall frieze in the State Dining Room. The other pieces have a gilt outer border with a wider pale yellow border on which are raised white enamel designs inspired by architectural motifs in the State Dining Room,

East Room, and Diplomatic Reception Room. The north view of the White House appears on the border of the dinner plate; the south view is on the border of the dessert plate.

This is the first time a new state service has been produced for the White House since the Reagan service of 1982. Supplemental pieces of the Woodrow Wilson and Franklin D. Roosevelt services were made by Lenox in 1995–96 and were a gift from the White House Historical Association. The new service is the fifth service that Lenox has been commissioned to manufacture for the White House. The first one—the first American-made service in the White House—was ordered by President and Mrs. Wilson in 1917.

DAWN · THE WHITE HOUSE · 2000 · Giclée Print

"The White House was conceived as and built to be a symbol of power for our country. This image was reinforced for me as I was painting on the South Lawn. The dawn broke, parting the storm clouds overhead—a fitting symbol for the dawning of a new century for this country and for this historic house."—Jamie Wyeth

A third-generation artist, Jamie Wyeth had his first one-man show in 1966. He became known for his controversial portraitures of icons such as President John F. Kennedy and fellow artist Andy Warhol. The animal life surrounding him on his farm in Pennsylvania and at his home off the coast of Maine has served as inspiration for paintings such as *Portrait of Pig, The Islander,* and *Ravens, Monhegan.* He created a series of drawings for *Harper's* magazine during the 1974 Watergate hearings and in 1976 painted a portrait of Jimmy Carter for the cover of *Time.* In 1981 and 1984 he painted Christmas cards for President and Mrs. Ronald Reagan. He was admitted into the National Academy of Design in 1969 and was appointed as a council member of the National Endowment for the Arts in 1972. Wyeth's work is included in many public collections, including the National Gallery of Art, National Portrait Gallery, Museum of Modern Art, Brandywine River Museum, John F. Kennedy Library, and the Farnsworth Museum.

John Adams

PAIR OF VASES

This pair of gilded porcelain vases is decorated with *grisaille* portraits of George Washington and John Adams, the first two presidents of the United States. The portraits are based on an 1812 engraving of the paintings of Washington by Gilbert Stuart and Adams by John Singleton Copley. The backs of the two vases are decorated with the Great Seal of the United States, in burnished and matte gold. These portrait vases are distinctive in their execution and quality. As a pair they commemorate the administrations of Presidents Washington and Adams that witnessed the planning, construction, and occupancy of the White House.

French, about 1820. Painted and gilded porcelain, 12 3/4 in. high

CYLINDER DESK WITH BOOKCASE

This monumental cylinder desk and bookcase is one of the most
sophisticated and fully developed pieces of American furniture
of the neoclassical period. This form of desk, with a slide that pulls out
to create a writing surface as the cylinder cover recedes, owes its design
origins to continental European furniture makers of the 18th century.
In emulating this form, an unknown New York cabinetmaker exhibited
a level of workmanship that compares in quality to the work of master
cabinetmaker Duncan Phyfe of New York. A desk of this form by
Scottish-born Phyfe's shop, c.1815–20, is located in the Green Room.
Now a second outstanding New York cylinder desk stands in the Red
Room to grace the state floor.

New York, about 1830. Mahogany, with kingwood and striped maple,
gilded metal mounts, and pulls, mirror plate, and glass. 96 $^3/_8$ in. high.

Symposium

TWO HUNDRED YEARS AT THE WHITE HOUSE
1800-2000

ABIGAIL ADAMS

THE *White House*
HISTORICAL ASSOCIATION

JOHN ADAMS

When John and Abigail Adams settled into the President's House in November 1800, they established a tradition that every president and first lady has honored for two centuries. More important, within a few months President Adams stepped aside as the people selected a new occupant with a new political ideology. The first White House and political party transitions were accomplished peacefully. To commemorate the anniversary of these important events, the White House Historical Association and the National Park Service presented a symposium entitled "Two Hundred Years at the White House: Actors and Observers."

*The press awaits
the start of an event
in the East Room.*

The organizations brought together a host of distinguished authorities to examine
the roles of the White House as a working home and office from the perceptions of
"actors"—the president, first lady, first family members, executive office staff, and
residence employees—balanced against the views of "observers"—the media,
American citizens, and foreign visitors. The capacity audience learned how the house
and officeholder have become inseparable in the public mind. As chief executives
molded the physical structure to their needs, the White House served across time as
a symbol of national pride, a rallying ground, and a target of protest. Presidents and
their families have found the house to be an instrument of display and power, as
well as a safe haven. The symposium presented a sweeping view of two centuries of
life and work in the building that houses one of America's most hallowed
institutions.

TWO HUNDRED YEARS AT THE WHITE HOUSE: ACTORS AND OBSERVERS

NOVEMBER 14, 2000

JOSEPH J. ELLIS

WELCOME

Robert L. Breeden, Chairman and Chief Executive Officer. White House Historical Association

Robert G. Stanton, Director, National Park Service

Gregori Lebedev, Executive Vice President and Chief Operating Officer,
    U.S. Chamber of Commerce

WILLIAM SEALE

THE WHITE HOUSE IN 1800: A RESIDENCE FOR THE REPUBLIC

"The Restoration of 1800" Joseph J. Ellis, Ford Foundation Professor of History,
    Mount Holyoke College

"The First White House" William Seale, Historian and Author

"'Splendid Misery': Abigail Adams as First Lady" Edith Gelles, Senior Scholar,
    Institute for Research on Women and Gender, Stanford University

EDITH GELLES

THE COMING OF AGE OF THE WHITE HOUSE

"Privileged Access: The First White House Photographs" Clifford Krainik, Historian

"A Republican Queen in the People's Palace: Dolley Madison Creates the White House"
    Catherine Allgor, Assistant Professor of History, Simmons College, Editor,
    The Louisa Catherine Johnson Adams Papers

"Jackson and Van Buren: Democratic Tension and National Aspiration in the White House"
    Michael D. Henderson, Superintendent, Morristown National Historical Park,
    National Park Service

CLIFFORD KRAINIK

BETTY MONKMAN

CRISIS AND CIVIL WAR

"Views of Mr. Lincoln's White House" Betty C. Monkman, Curator, The White House

"The Lincoln White House" Jean H. Baker, Elizabeth Todd Professor of History,
  Goucher College

MICHAEL D. HENDERSON

EVENING REMARKS

"The Making of The American President" Philip B. Kunhardt III, Filmmaker

PHILIP B. KUNHARDT III

NOVEMBER 15, 2000

WELCOME

Neil W. Horstman, Executive Vice President, White House Historical Association

WILLIAM BUSHONG

THE WHITE HOUSE IN THE GILDED AGE

"Frances Benjamin Johnston's White House" William Bushong, Historian,
  White House Historical Association

"The Gold in the Gilded Age" Richard Norton Smith, Executive Director,
  Gerald R. Ford Foundation

RICHARD NORTON SMITH

THE IMPERIAL WHITE HOUSE

"Stagecraft: The Presidency in the American Century" Garry Wills, Professor of History,
  Northwestern University

GARRY WILLS

LYDIA TEDERICK

JOHN A. GABLE

ALLIDA BLACK

MARTHA JOYNT KUMAR

"Images of White House Life" Lydia Tederick, Assistant Curator, The White House

"Theodore Roosevelt's White House" John A. Gable, Executive Director,
Theodore Roosevelt Association

"Eleanor and Franklin: Partners in Politics and Crises" Allida Black, Research Professor of
History, The George Washington University at Mount Vernon College,
Director and Editor, *The Eleanor Roosevelt Papers*

THE RHETORICAL PRESIDENCY

"Theodore Roosevelt and the Revolutionary Rhetoric of Conservation" Douglas G. Brinkley,
Director, Eisenhower Center for American Studies, University of New Orleans

"White House Cartoons: Clifford Berryman of the Washington Post *and* Evening Star*"*
Katherine A. Brasco, Center for Legislative Archives, National Archives and
Records Administration

"History's Eye: White House News Photographers" Dennis Brack, White House News
Photographers Association

"Presidential Reality: If It Hasn't Happened on Television, It Hasn't Happened"
Martha Joynt Kumar, Director, White House 2001 Project, Professor of History,
Towson University

EVENING RECEPTION

The White House

NOVEMBER 16, 2000

WELCOME

Hugh S. Sidey, President, White House Historical Association, *Time Magazine*

WHITE HOUSE TRANSITIONS

"Changing of the Guard on Pennsylvania Avenue" Michael Beschloss, Historian and
    Author, Member, Board of Directors, White House Historical Association

THE ACTORS' VIEW: PANEL DISCUSSION

MODERATOR

Marlin Fitzwater, Press Secretary to President Reagan and President Bush

PANELISTS

Senator Howard Baker, Chief of Staff to President Reagan

Capricia Marshall, Deputy Assistant to the President, White House Social Secretary

Susan Porter Rose, Chief of Staff to Mrs. Bush

Gary Walters, Chief Usher, The White House

THE OBSERVERS' VIEW: PANEL DISCUSSION

MODERATOR

Hugh S. Sidey, President, White House Historical Association, *Time Magazine*

PANELISTS

Max Frankel, Former Executive Editor, *New York Times*

Douglas G. Brinkley, University of New Orleans

BIRTHDAY PARTY: THE WHITE HOUSE VISITOR CENTER

NOVEMBER 16, 2000

The U.S. Marine Band
in Performance

President John Adams,
portrayed by Steven Perlman

Abigail Adams,
portrayed by Rebecca Bloomfield

President-Elect
Thomas Jefferson,
portrayed by Bill Barker

President Calvin Coolidge,
portrayed by Jim Cooke

*John Adams and Thomas
Jefferson (portrayed by
actors) discuss the transition
of executive power at the
White House during the
concluding program of the
symposium.*

Education Programs

Adam Nagar's winning entry is a second-grader's birthday wish for the White House.

Working in partnership with two of the nation's most successful educational publishers, the White House Historical Association reached classrooms across America with the story of the birthday of the White House. Cobblestone Publishers dedicated issues of two history magazines to the White House. Subscribers to Scholastic Classroom Magazines received special news coverage, activity books, a classroom poster, and an invitation to enter a student contest at one of three age levels.

Adam Nagar, a second-grader from New York, created the winning White House birthday card. Emily Hankinson, a fifth-grader from North Wales, Pennsylvania, penned the winning song. The author of the winning essay was Edward Berry, a seventh-grader from Tarpon Springs, Florida. The three student winners, their teachers, and families

After a special tour of the White House, student winners Edward Berry (front row, far left) and Emily Hankinson (front row, far right), their families, and teachers, gather for a photograph in front of the north entrance.

won a trip to Washington, D.C., and enjoyed a special tour of the White House. Seven hundred runners-up received "The White House Is Our House: A CD-ROM Visit."

The association also created "The Learning Center" on its web site, complete with lesson plans and quizzes for grades K–12. In partnership with National History Day, the association sponsored a weeklong teacher institute on the American presidency.

Some pieces were made for English and French royal families such as that of King George II of England and King Louis XV of France, and others bear family crests of former owners such as the duke of Northumberland. There are contemporary American pieces in the collection, too. Margaret Thompson Biddle's monogram appears on dinner pl... Gorham in 1916 and goblets by Tiffany, 1907–47."

In 1960, the last year of the Eis... Eisenhower accepted...

ALL CASE CLOCK
...ffingham Embree, New York, c. 1800

...nnie Eisenhower accepted a donation
...f American federal furniture for the
...plomatic Reception Room in 1960
...ght), to begin a collection of American
...rniture of the highest quality from the
...riod when the White House was con-
...ructed. Those objects have been supple-
...nted over the years by additional
...ces such as a tall case clock with musi-
...l works and a French wallpaper
...iews of North America," in the room
...day (opposite)

THE
WHITE HOUSE
ITS HISTORIC FURNISHINGS & FIRST FAMILIES

BETTY C.

BRUCE WHITE

Commemoratives

The White House: Its Historic Furnishings and First Families

This book by Betty C. Monkman, curator of the White House, celebrates the 200th anniversary of the White House by telling the story of the many historic objects that each president and his family have acquired and used while living and entertaining there. With forewords by the first ladies, introduction by Wendell Garrett, catalog by William G. Allman, and photography by Bruce White, the book was co-published by the White House Historical Association and Abbeville Press. The most comprehensive survey ever published of the furnishings of the President's House, the book is illustrated with color photographs supplemented by historical views of the state rooms, furniture, silver, glass, porcelain, and textiles.

The 2000 Christmas Ornament

This annual Christmas Ornament of the White House Historical Association commemorates the 200th anniversary of the White House as the home of the president of the United States. The center stone rotates to portray two highly detailed white sculptural reliefs of the north and south elevations.

The White House

USA 33

White House Stamp and First-Day Cover

On October 18, 2000, the United States Postal Service issued a 33-cent stamp depicting the north elevation of the White House at night in the snow. One hundred twenty-five million stamps in self-adhesive panes of 20 were printed. The White House Historical Association also produced a special first-day cover, which was sold during the year.

The President's House, December 1800, Holiday Cards

The White House Historical Association anniversary cards recall the first holiday season spent in the White House in the year 1800. Artist Tom Freeman portrayed the scene of a December reception in his watercolor depicting the south front, which President Adams used as the main entrance.

Medallion

The United States Mint produced a 3 inch bronze commemorative medallion portraying John and Abigail Adams and the north entrance to the White House. Rendered after oil portraits by Gilbert Stuart, the images are surrounded by a depiction of the stone carving of the rose swag that adorns the north entrance of the White House. The reverse is a representation of architect James Hoban's 1792 north elevation design for the White House. It is surrounded by a wreath of oak and acanthus leaves, also inspired by stone carvings from the north door surround.

A commemorative medallion struck by the United States Mint was presented to the anniversary dinner guests and made available to the public in a limited edition.

Publications

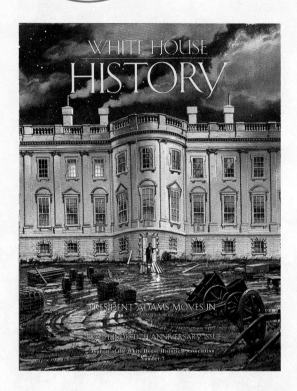

"President Adams Moves In:
Two Hundredth Anniversary Issue"
White House History, Number 7. The journal of
the White House Historical Association. Articles:
Abigail Adams as First Lady; The Midnight
Appointments; The White House in John Adams's
Presidency; John Adams: Farmer and Gardener;
Fashion in the Time of President John Adams;
The White House Collection: John and Abigail
Adams, A Tradition Begins.

Two Hundred Years at the White House:
Actors and Observers,
edited by William Seale. Collected papers from the
White House Historical Association Symposium,
November 14–16, 2000. Northeastern University
Press, forthcoming.

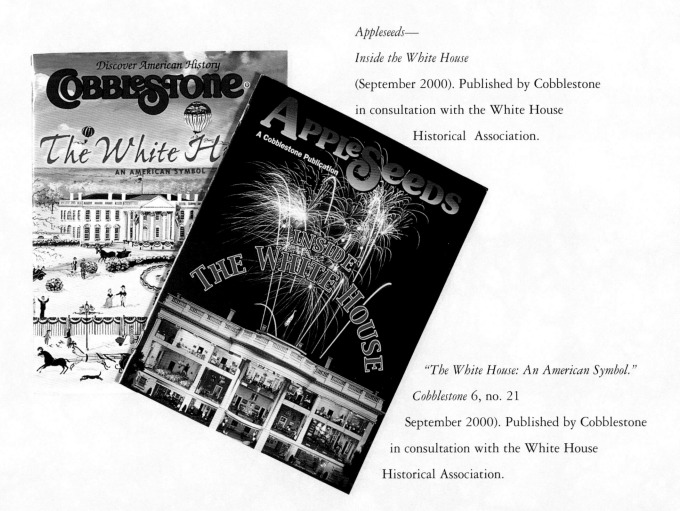

CHILDREN'S BOOKS

Appleseeds—

Inside the White House

(September 2000). Published by Cobblestone

in consultation with the White House

Historical Association.

"The White House: An American Symbol."

Cobblestone 6, no. 21

September 2000). Published by Cobblestone

in consultation with the White House

Historical Association.

Major Gifts

Since its founding in 1961, the White House Historical Association has significantly contributed to the fine and decorative arts collections in the White House. These objects were acquired so that they may be shared with the nation. A selection of major gifts follows.

KENNEDY

Mouth of the Delaware by Thomas Birch, oil on canvas, 1828

Desk and Bookcase, mahogany, c. 1785, Baltimore.

Ledger, March 1861, recording President Abraham Lincoln's initial appointments to military and civilian positions.

JOHNSON

Anna Eleanor Roosevelt Roosevelt by Douglas Chandor, 1949

James Madison by James Vanderlyn, 1816 (partial gift)

Armchair and Side Chair, mahogany, c. 1810, New York, possibly by Duncan Phyfe.

Linen Press and Desk, mahogany, c. 1790–1800, possibly Baltimore. Reportedly a gift to Dolley Madison's sister from President John Quincy Adams when he left the White House in 1829.

Argand Lamps, pair, bronze and cut glass, c. 1825–30, probably English, imported by Louis Veron, Philadelphia. Veron supplied lighting fixtures and other furnishings to the White House in the Andrew Jackson administration.

NIXON

Nevada Falls, Yosemite by Thomas Hill, 1889

Vernal Falls, Yosemite by Thomas Hill, 1889

Jacqueline Bouvier Kennedy by Aaron Shikler, 1970

John F. Kennedy by Aaron Shikler, 1970

Theodore Roosevelt by Tadé Styka, c. 1909

Tea Box, lacquered wood and wallpaper, c. 1811, China. Lined with samples of a French

    wallpaper from the President's House prior to the 1814 fire; given by Dolley Madison

    to Mrs. Benjamin Henry Latrobe, wife of the White House architect for Presidents

    Jefferson and Madison.

Tall Case Clock, mahogany, c. 1795–1805, Boston, case by John and Thomas Seymour.

Mixing Table/Stand, mahogany and marble, c. 1810–15, New York, labeled

    by Charles-Honoré Lannuier.

FORD

Rutland Falls, Vermont by Frederic Church, 1848

Lake Among the Hills (Lake Mohonk) by William M. Hart, 1858

James Hoban attributed to John Christian Rauschner, wax miniature, c. 1800

Abraham Lincoln by Augustus Saint-Gaudens, bronze, late 19th century

Armchairs, pair, mahogany, c. 1793–97, Philadelphia, attributed to Adam Hains.

    Possibly from George Washington's presidential residence in Philadelphia. (partial gift)

CARTER   **Dessert Coolers**, pair, porcelain, c. 1806, Paris, by Nast Manufactory.

From a James Madison family service.

*Lighter Relieving a Steamboat Aground by George Caleb Bingham, 1847

Sailing off the Coast by Martin Johnson Heade, 1869

Spring in the Valley by Willard Metcalf, c. 1924

Point Lobos, Monterey, California, by Thomas Moran, 1912

Benjamin Franklin by Jean-Antoine Houdon, bronze, c. 1778–1828 (partial gift)

Chandelier, cut glass, c. 1865–70, Birmingham, England, made by F.& C. Osler Co.

REAGAN   *George Washington* by Hiram Powers, marble, modeled 1838, carved 1840

John Adams by John Trumbull, c. 1792–93

Patricia Nixon by Henriette Wyeth, 1978

Drum Table, mahogany, c. 1800–10, New York, attributed to the workshop of Duncan Phyfe.

BUSH   *James Buchanan* by John H. Brown, watercolor on ivory, 1851

South Front of the White House by Jules Guérin, pencil on canvas on board, 1903

Sugar Bowl, silver, c. 1858, New York, made by Wood & Hughes.

From a 12-piece set purchased by former President Millard Fillmore in 1858 with funds from the sale of an 1850 presentation carriage.

CLINTON

Miss Lane's Reception by Albert Berghaus, pencil on paper, 1860–61

John F. Kennedy by William Draper, 1962

*Dolley Madison by Gilbert Stuart, 1804

Sand Dunes at Sunset, Atlantic City by Henry O. Tanner, c. 1886

Clinton State Service, 2000, made by Lenox, Inc., Trenton, New Jersey.

    To commemorate the 200th anniversary of the White House; place settings for 300.

Pier Table, mahogany, c. 1805–10, New York, labeled by Charles-Honoré Lannuier.

Vases, pair, porcelain, c. 1820, Paris. Gilded with portrait reserves of

    George Washington and John Adams.

Desk and Bookcase, mahogany, c. 1830, New York.

* Initial funding from the White House Historical Association.

ILLUSTRATION CREDITS